WILLIAMS OUTING CLUB

NORTH BERKSHIRE
OUTDOOR GUIDE

TEXT BY MEMBERS OF THE
WILLIAMS OUTING CLUB

Edited by Willard S. Morgan '96
2019 Revision by Daniel Gura '10

Map by Ethan B. Plunkett '00
and Patrick D. Dunlavey

WILLIAMSTOWN   MASSACHUSETTS

Please note: The Williams Outing Club assumes no responsibility for the safety of any users of this guide. It is understood that travel in the North Berkshire area involves certain risks and that the readers of this guide are liable for their own actions. Please read the Preparation sections carefully and expect the unexpected.

Williams Outing Club
North Berkshire Outdoor Guide
North Berkshire Trails

Book Design by Willard S. Morgan '96, Daniel Gura '10

Published by the Williams Outing Club
39 Chapin Hall Drive
Williams College
Williamstown, MA 01267

For ordering information contact the Williams Outing Club at the above address or by phone at (413) 597-2317.
Printed by GHP
West Haven, CT

Printed on recycled paper with soy-based ink.

Revised and updated 11th edition of the WOC Trail Guide.

ISBN 0-9669785-2-8

To Bob Hatton, who has spent more than half a century building trails in North Berkshire County. His paths have brought, and continue to bring, generations of us deeper into the woods.

CONTENTS

PHOTOS AND ILLUSTRATIONS

ODE TO THE GUIDE

Sons of the towns and cities,
Where'er your home abode,
Come straight unto my doorway
By steam or Trolley Road,
Glide swift on automobiles,
Walk up, or easier ride,
And you will better know me –
If you bring along this Guide.

Come not with rod or level,
With compass and with chain,
To measure heights and bases,
But coats to shed the rain;
Leave cameras behind you
My peaks and scars snap,
For you will best enjoy me
This Guide Book in your lap.

You may sleep upon my summit
With your head upon my breast,
The companion of my silence,
A partaker of my rest,
You may come with all your fixings,
And behold my every side,
But you'll never really know me
Unless you have this Guide.

From the *Pathfinder to Greylock Mountain*
The Berkshire Hills and Historic Bennington
By Col. W.H. Phillips 1910

ACKNOWLEDGEMENTS

Dozens of people have contributed to the completion of the *North Berkshire Outdoor Guide*, a book truly written by committee. The Williams Outing Club (WOC) and Williams College are not-for-profit, and much of the time devoted to this project was volunteered.

First, a thanks to all of the Williams students from years past who published the first ten editions of the *WOC Trail Guide*, starting with *The Mountains of Eph* in 1927. The eighth edition, edited by Jim Lerczak '88 and printed in 1988, provided the springboard for the greatly expanded ninth edition, produced in 1999 and edited by Willard Morgan '96. Many thanks to Ken Brown '05, who took on the challenge of updating the guide for its tenth edition in 2008.

The WOC Executive Boards from 1994 to 1999 contributed extensively through brainstormed ideas, field checking, and reading of draft material. Many other Williams students, WOC members or not, volunteered their time as well.

In a never-ending quest for answers to obscure questions regarding the North Berkshire area, a number of individuals stand out for offering their knowledge. Bob Hatton knows every twist and turn of trail in Williamstown and the Mt. Greylock State Reservation. He was quick to give help and advice. Paul Karabinos has combed the region for rock outcrops and accumulated a vast trove of information for exploring on- or off-trail in the North Berkshire area. Hank Art was always available to answer questions regarding natural history, environmental issues, or Hopkins Memorial Forest. Leslie Reed-Evans provided information on the Taconic Range, local trail initiatives and the Williamstown Rural Lands Foundation. Lauren Stevens shared his experience writing Berkshire County hiking and skiing guides. And, Dave Ackerson and Will Kirby '17 provided useful knowledge about rock climbing in the region.

Others have offered aid and constructive feedback on a series of drafts. Thanks again to Hank Art, Bob Hatton, Leslie Reed-Evans, and Dave Ackerson, as well as Cosmo Catalano, Helena Wartburg,

viii ACKNOWLEDGEMENTS

and Eric White. Kelsey Levine '10 helped with the tedious task of revising the index, and also with the less-tedious work of measuring and describing trails new to this edition.

Thank you to Cordelia Dickinson '98, who shouldered the burden of moving the ninth edition toward publication in 1997 and 1998. Corey effectively compiled all of the draft material into a manuscript and solicited reader feedback. Her careful research provided many of the numerous historical notes you will find scattered throughout this book.

Technological hurdles would have been insurmountable without the help of Sharron Macklin.

A project unto itself, the *North Berkshire Trails* map demanded the devotion of a committed cadre of students, and Ethan Plunkett '99 adopted the project as his own, painstakingly digitizing information from USGS maps and surveyed trails in the field. The greatest of thanks to Pat Dunlavey who refined the map data into a final form with his extensive professional cartographic experience.

Scott Lewis (WOC Director) has kept this project alive through a revolving Williams student body over more than two decades. He devised creative solutions to maintain progress despite the overcommitted student schedules. His paddling section is the most complete review of lakes, ponds, and rivers in the Berkshire area.

Thanks, in memory of Katie Craig '08, whose art appears in this book. Her enthusiasm and love for the outdoors have given enduring inspiration to many members of the Williams community.

We are grateful for the family of Bob Quay '04, who established the Bob Quay Memorial Fellowship that helps to support the WOC trail crew that maintains local trails during the summer weeks.

And finally, a special thanks to Bob and Leslie Nutting for their continued generosity to the Peter Ganyard 1950 Outing Club Fund, supporting our trails program and the reprinting of this guide.

INTRODUCTION

An infinite number of experiences await you in the North Berkshire area: on Stone Hill or Pine Cobble, in Hopkins Forest, throughout the Taconic or Greylock Ranges or along the Hoosic and Green Rivers. Best of all, these places are right out your door, accessible by foot, bike or a short car ride. Whether you are a student, resident, or visitor we encourage you to get out and experience the wonders around you.

The *North Berkshire Outdoor Guide* is a tool to facilitate your relationship with the land. We have designed this book with a progression that first introduces you to the area, basic safety, preparation, and outdoor ethics. Then a series of chapters describes the many easily accessible hiking trails close to Williamstown. Later, you will find information on winter activities, biking, fly-fishing, climbing, and paddling.

You need not be an athlete or seasoned outdoors person to explore the region, to experience the regenerative effects of a hike, to read the lessons of the landscape, or to encounter those spiritual moments of connection to the earth. Confidently match an activity to your comfort level and gradually increase the challenge over time. Remember to travel lightly, leave only footprints, and take only memories.

HOW TO USE THIS BOOK

The *North Berkshire Outdoor Guide* is a resource produced by the Williams Outing Club (WOC) as a service for Williams College students, Williamstown residents and the many year-round North Berkshire visitors. We have made every attempt to present the information in a clear and accessible manner. Please read on to learn how to navigate through the material included in this book.

ABOUT "NORTH BERKSHIRE"
Most guides to this area cover all of Berkshire County or a greater part of Massachusetts. In those publications "North County" usually refers to the Williamstown – North Adams – Mt. Greylock region.

This area is one with specific physiographic boundaries: The Dome to the North, the Taconic Range to the west, the Greylock Range to the south and the Hoosac Range to the east. "North Berkshire" seems an appropriate name for a logically defined area of Berkshire County with outdoor opportunities enough to earn its own guide.

ORGANIZATION
The Table of Contents lists chapter headings to guide you to general information categories such as "What to Bring," "Taconic Range," or "Biking." To find a specific trail or topic, refer to the index. A header on each page helps you find the information you need.

Progressions dominate the organization of information so that the reader can build logically through the book. Early chapters give a history of the area and prepare you to travel with safety, comfort and concern for the environment. Hiking trail descriptions follow, roughly in order of their distance from Williams College.

Other outdoor activities such as winter travel and mountain biking refer to earlier hiking trail descriptions and offer information for areas close to and then far away from campus. The paddling and climbing sections describe locations mostly beyond Williamstown due to a scarcity of local areas.

To further your outdoor knowledge and experience, an extensive Bibliography provides a list of titles and authors to pursue. A collection of Resources gives addresses, phone numbers and web sites of outdoor-related retail stores, local government and non-profit organizations and relevant national organizations.

TRAIL DESCRIPTIONS

The first eight editions of this book were exclusively trail and ski touring guides. Hiking trails remain the core information and fill over half of the text pages. The descriptions are written to be used with the included 15 x 24 inch map, *North Berkshire Trails*. As a result, a local map does not accompany the descriptions. The trails are grouped by geographic region in order of proximity to Williams: Local Walks, Stone Hill, Green Mountains, Taconic Range, The Hopper, Greylock North, Greylock West, Greylock Summit, Greylock East, and Greylock South.

For each trail you will see the following information:

TRAIL NAME

Distance: Field checked mileage, rounded to tenths, unless noted "(approximately)." Distances are one-way unless noted otherwise. Many trails may be combined into loops for longer hikes.

Estimated time: A rough estimate of hiking time for an average walking pace, not running, biking or skiing. Times given are one-way, unless indicated otherwise. Expect your times to differ somewhat from this figure. Does not include approach time by car or foot to the trailhead.

Blazes: Indicates the color of paint swatches or plastic pieces on trees to mark the trail.

Map location: A letter and number combination to find the trailhead with an index grid on the *North Berkshire Trails* map.

Maintenance: Name of the organization that maintains the trail. If the trail needs maintenance, contact it using information in the Resources section.

An introductory paragraph mentions points of interest or useful information about the described trail.

HOW TO GET THERE
- Bulleted list of directions with mileage to reach the trailhead.
- All directions begin from the roundabout at Field Park: the junction of Route 2 and Route 7 in Williamstown.
- Mileage, rounded to tenths and abbreviated, is given as cumulative figures from Field Park unless indicated otherwise.

DESCRIPTION
A route description with mileage (abbreviated mi.) as well as natural history and human history points of interest. Trails closest to Williams College are described in more detail than those distant. **Bold-faced** words are other trails or subjects covered in this guide that may be found through the index. A cross-reference is bolded only the first time it appears in the description. References in *Italics* may be found in the Bibliography.

ACCURACY
Every attempt has been made to provide accurate and complete information about outdoor activities in the North Berkshire area as of July 2018. Thanks to a very active outdoor recreation and land conservation community, new trails are built and old ones rerouted nearly every year. As a result, some information may become outdated. Always heed signs in the field or more current maps. To report changes or corrections, contact:

Williams Outing Club
Attn: Outdoor Guide
39 Chapin Hall Drive
Williamstown, MA 01267

HOW TO USE THE MAP

North Berkshire Trails has many advantages for outdoor enthusiasts in the Williamstown area. Parts of nine United States Geological Survey (USGS) 7.5 minute quadrangle maps have been combined into one area bounded by mountain ranges. From viewpoints in the area you can see much of the terrain portrayed on the map and identify features that interest you. Icons note trailheads, camping, canoe put-ins and fishing access points. For navigation, magnetic north lines have been printed in magenta and a one kilometer grid facilitates rough distance estimates.

CONTOUR LINES

If you are unfamiliar with topographic maps and contour lines, don't worry. You can use the other information at first and gradually learn how to read the elevation data to improve your navigation skills. A contour line (gray on this map) traces equal elevations along a hillside, as if water filled the valley to that level. A contour interval of 50 feet, approximately 15 meters vertically, separates each line. Practiced map readers can visualize a landscape from the squiggly mass of lines. If you are not there yet, at least use contours to determine the steepness of a route.

Think of a staircase with, let us say, 18 centimeter (about 8 inch) steps, one hundredth the height of our contour line steps. If the steps are far apart you have a gentle grade, maybe in a landscaped garden. On the other hand, if they are close together the stairs go straight up; envision the Mayan pyramids in Central America. Contour lines are like steps: when they are spaced apart (in broad valleys) you will have a gentle grade and when they are tight together (on hillsides), expect a steep climb.

USE OF ENGLISH UNITS

All distances in the text are given in English units: feet, yards or miles, and the map includes a miles scale. Most high points are labelled with metric and English elevation measurements.

INDEX GRID

Each trail description includes a "Map location" coordinate such as "L – 12" to find the trailhead. A grid of letters from west to east and numbers from south to north allows you to locate places within a one-kilometer square on *North Berkshire Trails*.

ACCURACY

All the elevation data and most political information (roads, buildings, etc.) derive from USGS topographical maps. Trails highlighted in pink have been field checked for accuracy and many were carefully surveyed for an exact location. Many features you find in the field, such as logging roads, may not be indicated on the map. At this scale of 1:50,000 we have shown only the most important information and left off other features to avoid clutter and improve readability. Never rely solely on this map as truth, use all your powers of observation to reconcile any discrepancies you find in the field.

THE WILLIAMS OUTING CLUB

When I went to college, I met for the first time with mountain scenery and it has yielded to me...the most skillfully concocted cup of physical and spiritual pleasures I have ever found anywhere in life.

John Bascom

HISTORY

In 1793, Williams College students lived in isolation from the outside world. The North Berkshire area legitimately constituted a sphere of its own and those living here knew the landscape well. Simple travel on foot or horse along narrow paths, carriage roads, or wood grades brought students and townspeople into close contact with the land every day. Mountain Day, an annual holiday from classes that originated in the early 19th century, freed students to explore the North Berkshire Hills or "Purple Valley."

In 1830, Williams students and professors led a crew of one hundred who cleared the Hopper Trail, previously a wagon road, three miles from Haley Farm to the summit of Mt. Greylock, in one day. Students also built a wooden tower on the summit that year, for sightseeing and scientific observation, and it was rebuilt and maintained into the 1850s.

Growing appreciation of mountains for their own sake found direction in the Alpine Club, founded in 1863 by professor Albert Hopkins. This was the first mountain climbing organization in the United States, before the White Mountain Club (1873) or Appalachian Mountain Club (1876). The Alpine Club stated its purpose:

To explore the interesting places in the vicinity; to become better acquainted...with the natural history of the localities, and to improve the pedestrian powers of the members.

The Club produced newsletters, recorded trip journals and named many features of the North Berkshire Hills.

A student government committee on "trails and byways" was organized in 1904, and a small group of undergraduates founded the current Williams Outing Club (WOC). WOC devoted its early years to winter sports, capturing the intercollegiate winter sports title in 1925, and encouraged interest in winter sports amongst Williams students in general.

In 1923, WOC took charge of the annual Winter Carnival, a major enterprise still organized and staffed by students. Held each February, the carnival includes biennial alpine and Nordic ski races, a snow sculpture contest with faculty judges, and an array of campus events. For several years the club ran an ice skating rink on Eph's Pond and a ski area at Sheep Hill, complete with three trails, a warming hut, and a 35-meter jump.

By 1927, the club had expanded its scope to include maintenance of hiking trails, intending to "open up all the previously neglected footpaths about Williamstown in order that those who so desire may tramp about the foothill." The first edition of the WOC Trail Guide, *The Mountains of Eph*, was published that summer.

To facilitate longer hiking and backpacking trips, WOC built several different cabins and shelters; the first was the Harris Memorial Cabin, located between Mount Williams and Mount Fitch (1932); only a chimney remains today. Currently, the club maintains the Jim Dorland '50 Memorial Cabin in Hopkins Forest, a 2600-acre educational and research facility owned by Williams College, as well as a lean-to near the tri-state marker.

After decades of faithfully serving the college community through trails and winter sports, WOC greatly expanded its definition of the word "outing" during the latter part of the 20th century to organize activities ranging from kayaking to rock climbing to farming.

WOC has also broadened its role as a service organization in the Williams College and Williamstown communities. Members teach physical education classes in which fellow students learn new outdoor skills and the instructors develop their teaching and leadership abilities. Other members organize a slate of day and overnight trips in the North Berkshires and throughout the northeast.

Each September, WOC runs the Williams Outdoor Orientation to Living as First-years (WOOLF), a program that provides four-day pre-orientation outdoors trips for new students. To demonstrate the unparalleled mountain access of Williamstown, many of the trips begin or end on campus.

Members (limited to the Williams College community) support WOC with an annual fee. Those who want to explore the Williamstown area on their own can borrow a wide variety of equipment from the Equipment Room and use resources in the WOC office. WOC is also responsible for the upkeep and supervision of the popular 2000-square-foot Nate Lowe Memorial Climbing Wall, which opened in 1995.

Few colleges have such a natural bounty of outdoor opportunities out their front door. The Williams Outing Club stands on the shoulders of Williams students who, since 1793, have plied the hills first by necessity, and then for study or pleasure. WOC has evolved from Professor Hopkins' Alpine Club and a small group of students promoting winter sports, to a large organization that encompasses more than one-third of the student body and a wide range of outdoor activities. Despite the inevitable changes of time, the mission of WOC remains true to the ideals of the Alpine Club 156 years ago:

…To stimulate participation and appreciation for outdoor activities…To further the ideal of college education, develop personal initiative and leadership, promote skills in outdoor recreation, educate itself and the college community about environmental conservation, seek new opportunities for outreach, and encourage the meeting of people with common interests.

WOC Constitution

MOUNTAIN DAY

Mountains of Eph, the first edition of the WOC Trail Guide, described Mountain Day as

> That day set apart by the Faculty to give the students the opportunity of becoming better acquainted with the mountains in the glory of the autumn foliage.

Today, hikes of varying lengths lead to a morning celebration of community and place on Stone Hill, and an afternoon celebration on Stony Ledge. There is also an all-campus picnic on the lawn outside the Paresky Student Center. Several hundred students, faculty, and staff members typically attend the festivities, which include refreshments and musical entertainment by campus groups at the three main event locations. The most important ideal of the day is to GET OUTSIDE, take time to look up at the surrounding beauty in the hills, and spend quality time with friends new and old!

The origin of Mountain Day is believed to date back to the early years of Williams when a day known as "Chip Day" was set aside each spring for students to clear the debris left over from the cutting and splitting of firewood during the winter. When Chip Day arrived in 1796, students subscribed to a fund and employed others to clean up for them. Freed from their task, they took the day as a holiday and spent it as they pleased.

Although Williams observed Chip Day throughout the first half of the nineteenth century, an additional holiday, soon known as Mountain Day, was granted so that students could go to the mountains, especially Mt. Greylock. The first recorded reference to Mountain Day is in President Edward Dorr Griffin's journal for 1827.

Student interest grew during the mid-19th Century, and the College instituted "Bald Mountain Day" (the original name of Stony Ledge) as well in 1857, when students first celebrated fall foliage from Stony Ledge. The Chapel chimes announced Mountain Day with the college's alma mater, "The Mountains," through the late-19th and early-20th centuries while interest waned. Among other activities, WOC always sponsored an overnight trip up Mt. Greylock.

In 1934, Mountain Day was officially abolished due to lack

of interest – only 40 students had participated the year before. Faculty members were afraid that if they gave students the day off, they would spend it in ways other than enjoying the outdoors.

By the 1960s, students began to advocate the resurrection of Mountain Day. A 1969 Williams Record editorial argued that such a holiday would "focus attention on our surroundings, which seem to go unnoticed by so many students." Williams finally resumed the celebration of Mountain Day in 1981. Held on the weekend, it was a great success: hikes, bikes, and bus rides brought community members to Stony Ledge, where festivities included cider and doughnuts, and musical performances.

Drawing on the popularity of Mountain Day, and recognizing its strength as both a community-building event and the importance of the landscape to the Williams experience, the college reinstated Mountain Day as a spontaneous holiday in 2000. On one of the first three Fridays in October, the chapel bells chime "The Mountains" and students are given the day off from classes to take part in an all-campus picnic and festivities at Stone Hill and Stony Ledge organized by the Williams Outing Club.

TRAIL WORK

Summer is the main season for building and maintaining North Berkshire County's hiking trails. Much of the work performed on these paths is the result of an ongoing partnership between the Williams Outing Club and the Williamstown Rural Lands Foundation. The Williamstown Conservation Commission also rallies volunteers to caretake hiking trails throughout the year.

The Robert Ikemori Quay '04 Outing Club Memorial Fellowship
In 2006, a fellowship was established by the friends and family of Bob Quay, a Williams College student killed tragically in a cycling accident soon after his graduation in 2004. Bob was an admired leader of the Williams Outing Club, and - more importantly - a passionate outdoorsman who enjoyed introducing others to the outdoors. The fellowship is awarded annually to an individual "committed to combining a sense of community service with enhancing accessibility to the local wilderness trails of Berkshire County." In this way, Bob's enthusiasm for encouraging others to enjoy the Berkshire hills continues on.

    If you are ever hiking in The Hopper, on the western slope of Mt. Greylock, take a moment to pause as you first cross Money Brook. Bob helped construct the foundation of this bridge during the spring of his senior year, just weeks before his death. The bridge now bears his name — a suitable tribute considering Bob's willingness to connect people and land.

Bob Quay '04

ORIGINS OF PLACE NAMES

ADAMS
After statesman and Revolutionary War hero Samuel Adams.

BENNINGTON
For Governor Benning Wentworth of New Hampshire.

BERKSHIRES
Named for a county in England, where the name is pronounced "Bark-sheer." A "shire" is an anglo-saxon administration district.

FITCH, MT.
For Ebenezer Fitch, the first president of Williams College.

GREEN MOUNTAINS
From the French "Vert mont" which means green mountain. This is also the derivation of "Vermont."

GREEN RIVER
Probably given because of the characteristic color of the water.

GREYLOCK, MT.
There are many versions of the story about how this mountain got its name. Some people believe that it was named for Waranoce, a Native American chief from Maine who was called "Gray Lock" by early settlers. Many historical references to wisps of cloud that often shroud Greylock's summit, and its "hoary aspect in winter," by writers and Williams College professors provide a more likely origin of the name.

HOOSIC
Derived from the Mohican Indian words "wujoo," meaning "a mountain," and "abic," meaning "a rock." The mountain range is spelled "Hoosac," the city "Hoosick," and the river "Hoosic."

HOPPER

Named for its resemblance to a grain hopper.

HOPKINS FOREST

After Amos Lawrence Hopkins, whose farm covered most of what is now the Massachusetts portion of the forest.

NEW ASHFORD

For the "new ash fort" constructed on the Cheshire-to-Williamstown stage road in 1750.

PITTSFIELD

Named for Sir William Pitt, the English statesman who befriended the colonies. His birthday coincides with the day in April 1761 that Berkshire County split off from Hampshire County.

STONE HILL

Refers to the quartzite outcrops once visible in many places from the valley below.

TACONIC

Either from the Indian names Taagh-ka-nick, meaning "water enough," or Tach-an-ni-ke, meaning "full of timber."

WILLIAMS, MT.

Named for Williams College and Ephraim Williams.

WILLIAMSTOWN

Named for Colonel Ephraim Williams, who willed his fortune to the town of West Hoosuck to help found a free school (Williams College), on the condition that the name be changed to Williamstown.

STARTING OUT

Common sense will take you a long way in the outdoors. Remember that you are responsible for your own safety, warmth, water, food, and shelter. The lack of modern amenities to provide these basic needs is part of what makes the outdoors so compelling.

For a short walk to Eph's Pond you have little to think about, perhaps an extra layer of clothing in the fall. On a couple-mile hike to Pine Cobble you will expend a bit more energy and climb to elevation where the weather may be different. A small pack with water, a snack, and an extra layer may suffice. An all-day trip on Greylock requires a few more items, and a multi-day backpack trip even more.

If you are new to the mountains, be conservative at first; let the simple information herein guide you, then seek out more information by attending organized trips or through literature referenced in the Bibliography. As you become accustomed to the Berkshire Hills let experience, knowledge, and fitness govern your judgements of what to bring. The old Boy Scout motto of "Be Prepared" does not mean you must have a mountain of gear on your back. Quite the contrary, be prepared with common sense, experience, sound knowledge, and a basic amount of equipment adjusted to the season as well as length and intensity of the excursion.

Most important, get out there and have fun. One thirsty or hungry trek will encourage you to bring water or food the next time. Experience will teach you more than any words in a book.

SAFETY

To avoid an "experience" of dangerous proportions, here are a few basic safety guidelines to follow. Always tell someone where you are going, especially if you go alone. If no friends are around, leave a note; that small gesture can save hours if you need assistance. Keep in mind how far you are from help and take responsibility for your own safety. A badly sprained ankle on Pine Cobble could mean a lengthy ordeal.

Adjust to the season and check the weather when possible;

storms may sweep in quickly to change conditions dramatically. From September to late December a series of hunting seasons in Massachusetts, Vermont, and New York make travel in the hills dangerous. Call the Outing Club, Department of Fisheries and Wildlife, or other relevant land management agencies for dates and information.

Please be careful if you are driving to a trailhead. Finally, keep aware towards the end of your trip when fatigue and eagerness to finish may cause an accident or lapse in judgement.

WHAT TO WEAR

Season, weather, the activity, and your intensity all affect how to dress on a given day. A "layer" system with attention to fabric types can make any trip a pleasure, whether hot and dry or cold and wet.

Heat (or lack thereof), wetness, and wind are the major factors that govern how to dress comfortably. Heat may emanate from the sun or your own body, precipitation and sweat introduce moisture, and wind causes evaporation and convective cooling.

Different fabrics offer various degrees of insulation, water repellency, and wind protection. A material insulates by trapping air in spaces either made by a weave or existing between layers. To protect against precipitation, a garment's fabric may be coated or laminated with a membrane that has microscopic pores. Waterproofed seams complete your rain protection. A tightly woven or lightly coated material may effectively block wind, but might not be waterproof.

Cotton is comfortable and insulates fairly well, but only when dry. When wet, all the air spaces collapse and convective cooling takes over. On a hot summer day, that feels great, but in winter cotton earns the title "death cloth."

Wool fibers retain a coating of oil that allow them to resist water saturation and maintain air spaces to insulate. For most of history, wool was the fabric of choice for outdoor activity during inclement weather.

However, since the early 1980s polyester and other synthetic fabrics have become the standard of outdoor clothing. Synthetic fibers are essentially plastic, a petroleum product, and resist moisture and insulate when wet, much like wool. Unlike wool, synthetics are not scratchy and may be customized into a myriad of products.

Informed layering can make any weather conditions manageable. The key is to regulate your body temperature, not too warm and not too cold. Aggressively vent by opening zippers or rolling up sleeves, and remove or add layers as necessary. Ideally, you learn how to adjust before you become hot or cold.

During cold weather, wetness is your greatest enemy, usually in the form of sweat. To avoid overheating, start cold; take off a layer before moving and your body will quickly warm up. Before you begin to sweat, vent and de-layer. At a rest break, quickly put on a jacket and hat to stay warm, and remove them before starting again.

Below is more information about a standard layering system for all but warm summer days.

BASE LAYER
(Next to the skin)
Long underwear. Synthetics wick moisture away from your skin and insulate when wet. No cotton!
INSULATING LAYER(S)
Fleece or wool shirt, sweater or jacket. Adjust thickness or number of layers to weather.
SHELL
Windproof and water-resistant at least. Waterproof best. There are many options, so shop around. Waterproof/breathable works best and stops rain, and water vapor from your body goes out (mostly).

You can layer your torso, lower body, feet, hands, and head individually. If you don't have a lot of fancy wool or synthetic clothes, work with what you have, but realize you have to be much more diligent to avoid sweating and losing your insulation.

FOOTWEAR

As with clothing and equipment, adjust your footwear to the demands of an activity. Sneakers or even sandals are fine for local walks. Once on mountain trails, boots offer greater foot and ankle protection. Lightweight leather and fabric models are fine for most hikes. On an overnight trip, stiffer boots reduce the likelihood of spraining an ankle with a heavy pack. In winter, insulated or double boots keep your feet warm and dry.

Beware of new boots, which often don't fit properly, or need to be broken in. Try to break in new boots *before* heading out into the woods by wearing them around town. Wear two pairs of socks: a smooth liner sock and a thick wool sock to reduce friction and blisters. If you feel a "hot spot" from rubbing, stop, adjust your socks and lacing or put on moleskin to prevent a blister. On an overnight trip, bring a pair of comfortable camp shoes to relax in.

HYDRATION

Drink water, and lots of it. A field measure of adequate hydration is "clear and copious," regarding your urine. On an overnight trip, that means between three and five quarts per day, more for high exertion or winter activities. Proper hydration helps body temperature regulation, food metabolism and muscle endurance. Carry at least one full water bottle on any excursion.

WHAT TO BRING

Your brain is the most important tool in the outdoors! Remember "common sense," too, and bring plenty of it. If you are reading this information, you are on the right track; a few basic tips can shortcut a long learning curve of mistakes. Below is a series of equipment lists for trips relating to the trails described in this guide. WOC members can borrow many of the following items from the WOC Equipment Room.

LOCAL WALKS
- Weather-appropriate clothing (see "What to Wear")
- Extra layer – Sweater, fleece, or windbreaker

SHORT HIKES
Stone Hill, Hopkins Forest, Pine Cobble, etc.
- All items for Local Walks, plus:
- Full water bottle
- Snack
- Small daypack or hip pack
- Trail guide and map

HALF-DAY HIKES
Dome, Hopper, Taconic Range trails
- All items for Short Hikes, plus:
- Extra food
- Sun protection – Hat, sunscreen and sunglasses
- Pocketknife – A thousand uses
- Rain gear – Even on a sunny day
- Compass – If you know how to use one
- Flashlight or headlamp – Just in case
- First aid supplies
- Hiking boots (see Footwear)
- Thick wool or synthetic blend socks

FULL-DAY HIKES
Mt. Greylock, loops with several trails
- All items for Half-Day Hikes, plus:
- Second full water bottle
- Lunch
- More first aid supplies
- Whistle – For emergency
- Hat and gloves – Essential any time of year
- Small tarp – To sit on or for an emergency shelter

OVERNIGHT HIKES
Anywhere in the area or beyond
- All items for Full Day Hikes, plus:
- Extra socks – Keep feet warm and dry
- Backpack – Internal or external frame
- Sleeping bag – Appropriate temperature rating
- Sleeping pad – Insulates you from cold ground
- Shelter – Tent, tarp or bivy sack
- Camp shoes – Sandals or old running shoes
- Ground tarp – Under tent or sleeping pad
- Food – See below
- Stove – Fires are restricted in most areas
- Fuel – Appropriate to stove
- Matches or lighter
- Cooking pot and grips (to avoid burning skin/clothes)

OVERNIGHT HIKES (continued)
- Cup, bowl and spoon
- Toilet paper and trowel – See "Sanitation"
- Toiletries – Toothbrush and toothpaste
- Trash bags – To keep clothes dry
- Rope – To hang food away from animals
- Camera
- Journal

WINTER
- All items for Day Hike or Overnight, plus:
- Mittens, shell mittens, or both
- Balaclava or neck gaiter
- Liner socks – Reduce moisture, help insulate
- Gaiters – Keep snow out of boots
- Layer clothing system (See above)
- Wool sock to insulate water bottle
- Thermos
- Down or synthetic-fill jacket

FOOD

> "I think," said Christopher Robin, "that we ought to eat all our provisions now, so we won't have so much to carry."
>
>   - A. A. Milne

Common sense extends to fueling your body during sustained outdoor activity. For a short hike, grab a piece of fruit or a granola bar. On long day and overnight trips, the primary guideline is to eat a lot. Your body may not be used to so much exertion or the demands of weather. Always pack a little extra food, just in case something unexpected happens. In the winter, it is a great idea to carry a hot drink with lots of sugar in it, in case you need to warm people up!

The most important factors to consider when selecting food for an extended trip are energy content, weight, preparation time and taste. Below is a list of useful staples and ingredients to help you decide what to take. Before leaving, repackage as much food as possible in sturdy plastic or Ziploc® bags, in order to minimize weight, volume, and the amount of garbage you will have to carry out with you. Try snacking all day on the trail instead of eating a big lunch. Your body will thank you. On short trips you can carry less dried foods. Be creative!

SNACKS
Granola bars, fruit, dried fruit, energy bars, nuts, trail mix (peanuts, raisins, nuts, chocolate chips, etc.), chocolate, fig newtons

LUNCH
Bagels, pita bread, tortillas, crackers, peanut butter, almond butter, jam, cream cheese, hummus mix, cheese, carrots, pepperoni, tuna

BREAKFAST
Hot cereal, cold cereal, dried milk, potato flakes, powdered eggs, pancake mix, dried fruit

DINNER
Pasta, sauce mixes, rice, beans or bean flakes, couscous, fresh vegetables (onion, pepper, cabbage, carrots), cheese, soup mix, sun-dried tomatoes, sunflower seeds

DESSERT
No-bake cheesecake, pudding (shake to mix in Tupperware® or water bottle), cookies

EXTRAS
Spices (salt, pepper, fresh garlic, oregano, basil, cumin, curry, cinnamon, brewers yeast), hot sauce, salsa, cooking oil, soy sauce, butter or margarine, baking mix, honey, cocoa, tea, drink mix with vitamin C

For more ideas about backcountry cooking and nutrition refer to the *NOLS Cookery*.

OUTDOOR TRAVEL

You are at the trailhead, maybe for a long day hike or perhaps an overnight trip. A note with your itinerary is at home, and a pack with water, food, clothes, and some odds and ends hangs on your back. But you have a few questions: What do two paint marks on a tree mean? Should I take this short-cut trail up the steep hill? Where should I camp? How about a fire? What if I sprain my ankle? What should I do about trash along the trail? Uh-oh, I need to go to the bathroom.

This section is designed to help you explore the outdoors safely and responsibly. The information is an introduction, not a comprehensive how-to manual. Refer to titles in the bibliography like *Soft Paths* for more complete descriptions of outdoor travel.

As you head outdoors, remember: it is a fragile place. You should take steps to minimize your impact on the land in order to preserve its delicate ecosystems. Every aspect of your trip — from planning where to hike and camp, to determining what to bring and how to clean up after yourself — should take into account your impact and how you can lessen it through best practices and techniques.

Taking a conscientious approach will maintain the land's integrity and allow long-term enjoyment by you and those who follow. The Leave No Trace™ Program is a nationwide campaign that provides the latest information about how to travel in nature with the smallest possible footprint. It is certainly worth visiting leavenotrace.org to learn more about how to respect the outdoors while you're out there enjoying it.

Finally, a note about cell phones. Many hikers bring cell phones on the trail to navigate, snap photos, or as a way to contact help in case of an emergency. **Carrying a phone should not take the place of proper preparedness.** It is fully possible that your phone battery might fail, and there are also many hikes in this guide that take you to places without cellular service.

HIKING

Most of the time we are outdoors, we are walking, running, or riding on trails. To help prevent erosion and preserve the beauty of the landscape, avoid widening trails. If the trail is muddy, wear waterproof boots and gaiters, and plow through the mud. If it's rocky, don't seek a smooth path alongside the trail's edge. Tempting as it may be in some situations, do not cut switchbacks or start other shortcuts of your own.

When you are estimating the mileage you plan to cover, keep in mind the fitness level of your group, as well as the nature of the terrain. Accidents tend to happen when people are traveling at an uncomfortable pace or at the end of the day. Know when it will get dark, and select your starting time with that in mind. Keep your speed consistent and stay together. If you spread out, be sure to stop and regroup at all trail junctions to avoid separating.

Besides using existing footpaths, traveling off-trail is an option in some places. Backcountry areas are often rewarding to explore, but you should visit them only if you are confident in your navigation skills and your ability to minimize your ecological impact.

If you are traveling off-trail with a large number of people, plan to hike in parties of not more than six, and choose your route carefully to avoid fragile terrain and critical wildlife habitat. The most durable surfaces for traveling are rock, gravel, and sand, which you can usually find along rivers and streams. When hiking on vegetation that will recover from mild trampling, spread out across the hillside. Do not walk on fragile vegetation.

During winter, frozen ground and snow-cover dramatically reduce your impact. However, the spring thaw brings sloppy mud and a limit to low-impact off-trail travel.

NAVIGATION

That most-important tool comes into play again! Be alert and observant when travelling in the outdoors. Make mental notes of notable landmarks, changes in terrain, junctions with old woods roads, a cascading waterfall, or a beautiful hemlock grove. Every once in a while, look behind you: a place can be unrecognizable from another angle three hours later. If you are observant, you should at least be able to return the way you came.

To follow a particular route, use the tools available. Carry a trail guide and at least one map of the area. Learn how to read a topographic map and then to use a compass. Familiarize yourself and your group with the route you will be taking, as well as the locations of the nearest road should you need it. While you are on the trail, be sure to check your map periodically, so you will know where you were last if the group gets lost. Nearly all the trails in this guide are marked with painted or plastic color blazes on trees to help you follow the route. A double blaze, one above the other, marks a turn in the trail. Most trail junctions have signs; they are a great way to confirm your location on a map.

WEATHER

> If you don't like the weather in New England, wait
> five minutes.
> - Mark Twain

While this oft-quoted pronouncement is a bit of an exaggeration, weather in the Berkshires can be variable, particularly at higher elevations. Check the forecast before you head out, especially for an overnight or winter trip. While out, stay alert for signs of a change in weather. High thin clouds signal the passage of a front within the next twenty-four hours, and a strong wind often precedes a warm or cold front.

FIRST AID

The three most important rules for wilderness first aid are prevention, prevention, and - you guessed it - prevention. Be sure to read the section "Starting Out" for information on appropriate equipment to bring and other preventative considerations. Generally, be conservative in any risky situations and stay well fed and hydrated. Injuries and medical emergencies in the outdoors are more serious because hospital care is often hours away. Thankfully, emergencies are rare and more often we encounter cuts, blisters, dehydration, fatigue, mild hypothermia, or sprains.

Common sense can help you treat these minor conditions on short hikes until you get home. On overnight trips you will want to have more knowledge (see Bibliography) or a first aid course. The Red Cross offers first aid courses in most communities. If you plan to spend a lot of time in the outdoors consider taking a wilderness medicine course offered by organizations such as SOLO or Wilderness Medical Associates (see Resources).

If you do have an emergency situation, above all, stay calm and do not create a second victim through haste or carelessness. Administer first aid as you have learned or been trained, and go for help. If you have enough people, do not leave the patient alone and have more than one runner leave to call for assistance.

EMERGENCY PHONE NUMBERS

For a life-threatening emergency in Vermont and Massachusetts, call **911**.

For a non life-threatening emergency, call one of the following numbers:

• Williamstown Police Department	(413) 458-5646
• North Adams Police Department	(413) 664-4945
• North Adams Regional Hospital	(413) 664-5000
• Berkshire Medical Center	(413) 447-2000

Williams College students can call Williams College Security for a non life-threatening emergency at (413) 597-4444. Ask them to get in touch with the Williams Outing Club.

CAMPING

A night outdoors requires more planning than a simple day hike does, but the rewards are often great. Refer to the "Starting Out" section for information on clothing, equipment, and food. During a night out, you become a self-sufficient being with a house on your back, though hopefully one that is not too heavy!

Most public lands in the North Berkshire area limit overnight stays to shelters, designated tent sites, or campgrounds. This policy concentrates impact in specific places to preserve a greater land area. Vermont's Green Mountain National Forest allows dispersed camping (see page 27 for details). If you travel elsewhere in New England, check local regulations before you go.

There are a number of actions that you must take in order to conduct yourself responsibly during a night afield, particularly with regard to food and garbage management, fires, water, and human waste disposal.

FOOD AND GARBAGE

After meals, wash all of your dishes and cookware at least 200 feet from any water source. Strain dirty dishwater (using an old piece of window screen, cheesecloth, etc.) to remove food particles, and pack these out. Scatter dish water over a wide area.

All food items (food, cookware, utensils), garbage, and personal care items need to be stored well off the ground at night to keep animals from getting to them. This is usually done by hanging a 'bear bag.' A proper bear bag setup requires practice and you should consider a dry-run before heading into the woods! Lightweight rope or cord is essential, and knowledge of various knot-tying techniques will be helpful. In general, items should be stored in a stuff sack, duffel bag, or sealed plastic bag and hung from a tree trunk at least 16 feet above ground and eight feet from the trunk.

FIRES

What is more enjoyable than a warm campfire after a taxing day on the trail? Campfires – once as much a part of the outdoor experience as sore feet – are now discouraged for a number of reasons. Carelessly built fires leave blackened scars on the forest floor, lessen the soil's ability to hold moisture, and burn away nutrients essential for plant growth. If you are camping in an area where no fires have been built before, you should not build one unless it is absolutely necessary. Carry a camp stove and adequate fuel for cooking your food, as well as enough warm clothing to prevent you from having to rely on a blaze for warmth.

If you are camping in an area where fires are permitted and you do decide to build one, use preexisting fire rings or Leave No Trace techniques. Books such as *Soft Paths* describe how to build a low impact mound fire. Collect only pieces of wood that can be broken by hand and do not break dead branches off standing trees. Do your wood gathering before dark, so that you can locate areas that have not been picked clean by other travelers and avoid trampling vegetation unnecessarily.

WATER

Although the 1927 edition of this guide noted, "Any of the springs and brooks up in the mountains about Williamstown are safe for drinking purposes," this is no longer the case. **You must filter or chemically treat water from backcountry sources.** Drinking unpurified water may lead to ailments such as giardia, an intestinal illness that causes intense and unpleasant bowel problems. Water can be purified through several methods. Be sure to follow instructions when using chemical treatment or filtration systems, and always plan a back-up water purification option in case your first choice fails.

IODINE OR CHLORINE TABLETS
MIXED-OXIDANT SOLUTIONS
COMMERCIAL FILTERS
ULTRAVIOLET LIGHT
BOILING
   Be sure to account for stove fuel use if using this method.

   Throughout your trip, make sure that you, and everyone with you, drinks water constantly. Staying properly hydrated can prevent many common backcountry ailments. Three-to-five quarts a day is the minimum amount recommended to replace lost fluids. Drink enough to make your urine clear and copious.

SANITATION & WASTE DISPOSAL

You should be prepared to carry out everything you carry in, including paper, plastic, metal, and food scraps. Plan ahead by repackaging food to cut down on waste, and bring trash bags that you can seal shut. Make it a habit to pick up any trash that you see, whether or not it is yours.

   When you relieve yourself in the woods, there are some definite do's and don'ts. Urine is mostly water and salts, and is not generally harmful to the environment when dispersed. Feces, on the other hand, can transmit waterborne diseases such as giardia. Human waste should be disposed of in a way that reduces environmental and aesthetic impacts.

   Urinate off-trail and away from campsites. Most public lands in the Williamstown area have outhouses at shelters and campgrounds. Use them when possible. When there is no outhouse for feces, dig a small hole about six inches deep (in the organic soil), at least 200 feet from water, trails, and campsites. Bring a trowel or improvise a tool, such as your boot heel or a stick to excavate a hole. Avoid gullies that may fill with water in the next heavy rainfall.

After use, stir in some soil with a stick to facilitate fecal decomposition, and cover with soil and duff. If possible, avoid traditional toilet paper and experiment with natural objects like leaves, smooth stones, or snow. If you must use toilet paper, note that it decomposes too slowly to bury, and burning it increases the risk of forest fires. Instead, carry it out in a sealed plastic bag, and please do not leave little white "flags" to mark your spot.

PUBLIC LANDS & REGULATIONS

The following are general guidelines for the principal areas described in this guidebook. Since specific regulations change frequently, it is best to call for updated information before heading out.

APPALACHIAN TRAIL
- Camping permitted only at designated sites.
- Shelters are "first come, first served." Groups should not use them during the high-season (June-October) and should plan on using tents instead.
- All vehicles prohibited, including mountain bikes.

GREEN MOUNTAIN NATIONAL FOREST
- Dispersed camping allowed except within 200 feet of a road, trail, Forest boundary, or water.

GREYLOCK RESERVATION, CLARKSBURG STATE FOREST, AND TACONIC TRAIL STATE PARK
- Camping allowed only at designated sites.
- See "Appalachian Trail" above regarding shelters.
- Campground sites require a reservation:
  (1 (877) I-CAMP-MA or visit www.ReserveAmerica.com)
- No alcoholic beverages.
- Mountain biking on designated trails only.

HOPKINS MEMORIAL FOREST
- No camping or fires of any kind allowed.

- All vehicles, including mountain bikes, prohibited.
- To obtain a permit for group use and/or collection of any natural material, contact the Center for Environmental Studies at Williams College.

NATURAL HISTORY

A hike in the North Berkshires can be more than just an exercise of the legs, or a journey from trailhead to summit. If you keep an eye out, you can also learn something about how the area has come to look the way it does. Natural history includes every aspect of the study of the landscape, from minute details like dispersal of seeds by ants from spring flowers to grand events like the advance of glacial ice sheets. Knowing how to read signs of forest succession, tracking animals through fresh snow, and understanding the forces that shaped the mountains can help you expand your knowledge and use of the outdoors.

GEOLOGY

The Berkshire Hills are part of the Appalachian Mountain Range, one of North America's old mountain systems. Between 500- and 250-million years ago, three collisions between North America and other land masses, such as Africa, created mountain ranges that may have been as massive as the modern Rocky Mountains. The intense heat and pressure of these collisions metamorphosed the involved rock into new forms.

Common rocks of the North Berkshires are all metamorphic. Marble, formerly limestone, underlies the Hoosic River valley. Quartzite, formerly sandstone, is in scattered locations such as Stone Hill and Pine Cobble. Phyllite and schist, formerly silt and mudstone, compose much of the Taconic, Greylock, and Hoosac Ranges. As mountains formed, erosion gradually wore down the landscape over time, and water carried sand and silt to the oceans.

Ice ages have come and gone numerous times in "recent" geologic history, measured in millions of years! The last ice age completely covered New England as far south as Long Island and Nantucket only 20,000 years ago. As ice retreated northward through the North Berkshires about 14,500 years ago, it dammed the Hoosic River and formed a giant body of water, Lake Bascom. This lake filled the entire valley to an elevation of 1,045 feet, almost

500 feet deep in places! Within 500 years, the ice and lake were gone and vegetation returned, to mature in response to gradual global warming over thousands of years.

SETTLEMENT & SUCCESSION

The next significant change in Berkshire County's landscape came at the hands of white settlers. By 1830, over 70% of the woods surrounding Williamstown had been logged or cleared for farming. With the opening of the Erie Canal in 1825, however, the poorer farmers began moving west in search of more productive land and abandoned their fields, while the more prosperous farmers remained and bought up the land. Eventually the land gave way to the processes of forest succession.

This ecological cycle begins with the colonization of open areas by fastest-growing, fast-dispersing "pioneer" species, a group that in this region is dominated by "puckerbrush," a tangled thicket of shrubs and young trees. Eventually, hardier and more shade-tolerant species appear among the aging colonizers. The seedlings of the colonizers cannot withstand the increased shade, so as the older individuals die, they fail to replace themselves. Over time, this produces a shift from flash-in-the-pan colonizers to slower-growing but longer-lived species.

Today, although you can see the foundations of old farmhouses and crumbling stone walls in many formerly cultivated areas, seventy five percent of the regional landscape is again covered with trees.

FLORA & FAUNA

Above 2,500 feet, boreal forests of mostly red spruce and balsam fir dominate because of more severe weather conditions. At most lower elevations, deciduous forests reign. The most common trees on the north and east facing slopes are sugar maple, beech, yellow birch, white birch, ash, cherry, and hemlock. On south and west facing slopes, oaks and hickory are prevalent. However, relative abundance of various species may differ as a result of a wide variety of factors, including the land-use history of a particular area.

Red maple dominates former pastureland, paper birch and bigtooth aspen favor areas once used for growing crops, and rows of sugar maple and red oaks can often be found along the edges of abandoned carriage roads and woodlots. The presence of longer-lived species like beech, sugar maple, and hemlock, in terms of succession, represent stands in their climax stages, which can also be distinguished by a much more diverse range of tree sizes and ages.

Northern hardwoods provide the spectacular display of fall colors that attract visitors from all over the country. In the spring and summer, they also harbor a number of stunning wildflowers, particularly the early-blooming spring ephemerals, which bloom and wither before the trees leaf out.

Common mammals in the Williamstown area include white-tail deer, eastern gray squirrels, red squirrels, eastern chipmunks, eastern cottontail rabbits, mice, shrews, moles and voles, as well as opossums, woodchucks, and porcupines. Those who are on the trail at dawn or dusk may see more wildlife and less common species such as gray foxes, or moose. Rare mammals include bobcat and river otters.

Reforestation has brought an increase in the population of both black bears and coyotes. Neither poses a serious danger to people; they generally flee at the sight or smell of humans, but coyotes can be a threat to small domestic animals. Keep your eyes open to see what you find out there.

For more information refer to *Farms to Forest*, *North Woods*, *Eastern Forest*s or other sources listed in the bibliography.

Birch bark drawing by Katie Craig '08

INTRODUCTION
TO HIKING

There is something unnatural about walking. Especially uphill, which always seems to me not only unnatural, but so unnecessary. That iron tug of gravitation should be all the reminder we need that in walking uphill we are violating a basic law of nautre...[Yet] there are some good things to say about walking...It stretches time and prolongs life...I have a friend who's always in a hurry; he never gets anywhere. Walking makes the world much bigger, and therefore more interesting. You have time to observe the details...

- Edward Abbey

HIKING

An enormous number of hiking trails and old logging roads can be found in the Williamstown area. They include everything from gentle strolls along cool mountain streams to steep ascents with breathtaking views of the surrounding mountain peaks. For those who want to spend a longer period of time outdoors, there are a variety of shelters and campsites, both accessible and remote. This section focuses on those trails that can be reached on foot or within a drive of fifteen minutes or less. Rather than outlining complete routes, we have chosen to describe individual trails and how they connect with each other, so that you can design your own adventures. A list of some favorite WOC hikes appears on the following pages.

The trail descriptions are divided into sections: **Local Walks**, **Stone Hill**, **Green Mountain**, **Taconic**, and **Greylock**. The first section and Stone Hill describe a few smaller areas that are located within, or immediately adjacent to, the central part of Williamstown. The Green Mountain section covers the area to the north, including a portion of the Appalachian and Long Trails. The Taconic section is comprised of the Taconic Range that stands to the west of Williamstown, and the Greylock section covers the

Greylock Range, which is situated to the southeast. Each description includes directions to the trailhead and an explanation of the route, as well as comments on possibilities for other outdoor recreation like mountain biking and cross-country skiing. There is also a listed "hiking time" for each trail, which is based on the formula used in AMC's *White Mountain Guide*: one half-hour for every mile of walking, and one half hour for every thousand feet of elevation. Once you have hiked a few trails, and compared your actual hiking times to the listed ones, you should be able to estimate how long it will take you to hike any other trail in the book. Within each chapter, hikes are arranged in order of their proximity to the center of Williamstown.

When setting off on a hike of any length, remember that good preparation is essential for your comfort and safety. Be sure to read the introductory sections of this guide, which deal with issues like first-aid and traveling in the outdoors. Always check the weather before you head out, and leave a copy of your itinerary with friends. Respect your own limits, and those of your group–remember, the mountains will still be there next week or next month. Above all, have fun exploring this extraordinary place!

DEER HUNTING SEASON

If you venture into the woods for any reason during late fall, exercise extreme caution. Wear brightly colored (but not white) clothing and consider carrying a string of bells to jingle as you walk. The most dangerous seasons for hikers are the rifle and shotgun seasons, but it is also important to be aware of the seasons for bow-hunting and muzzle-loaders, which occur around the same time. The approximate dates for local hunting seasons follow:

MASSACHUSETTS
Shotgun Season: Fourth week in November to mid-December

NEW YORK
Rifle Season: First Monday after November 5 to first Tuesday after December 7

VERMONT
Rifle Season: Second half of November.
Muzzle Loader Season: Second week in December.

For the exact dates of the deer hunting seasons in any given year, contact one of the agencies listed below:

Massachusetts Department of Fish and Game
    www.mass.gov • (617) 626-1500
New York Department of Environmental Conservation
    www.dec.ny.gov • (518) 402-8845
Vermont Fish and Wildlife Department
    www.vtfishandwildlife.com • (802) 828-1000

RECOMMENDED HIKES

The sixty-odd trail descriptions that follow may be overwhelming to those new to the North Berkshire area. Here are some recommended hikes to get you started. Enjoy!

SHORT HIKES (< 4 hours)
    Berlin Mountain (Class of '33) Trail
    Berlin Pass Trail
    Phelps Trail–Taconic Crest Trail–Mill's Hollow Trail
    Hopkins Forest Loop
    Pine Cobble Trail
    Stone Hill Loop Trail
    Overlook–Hopper–Appalachian Trails
    Stony Ledge–Roaring Brook Trails
    Roaring Brook–Deer Hill Trail
    Hopper Trail–Haley Farm–Sperry Road

LONGER HIKES (4 hours +)
    R.R.R. Brooks–Shepherd's Well–Taconic Crest–Birch Brook Trails
    Broad Brook–Agawon–Dome Trails
    Pine Cobble–Appalachian–Broad Brook Trails
    Hopper–Money Brook–Mount Prospect Trails
    Old Adams Road–Appalachian–Cheshire Harbor Trails

LOCAL WALKS

Several areas near campus and the commercial district are convenient for a short stroll or picnic lunch on a warm, sunny day. Each location will encourage you to appreciate Williamstown's and Williams College's proximity to natural places. So put on your shoes and explore! Your car will be useful to reach trails described later.

EPH'S POND
Distance: Short walk
Estimated time: Your choice
Blazes: None
Map location: I – 20
Maintenance: Williams College

Named after Colonel Ephraim Williams, whose bequest started the Free School that became Williams College, Eph's Pond is a great place to observe birds or a magnificent view of the ranges around Williamstown.

HOW TO GET THERE
On foot from campus, students walk north, towards Mission Park and the tennis courts, then down Stetson road past the field house and downhill toward Cole Field.
- By car, drive east on Route 2 from Field Park to Park St., the second road on your left (0.2 mi.).
- Turn onto Park St., and follow it north 0.3 mi. to Lynde Lane.
- Turn right (east) onto Lynde Ln. (0.5 mi.) and then left (north) on Stetson Road at the tennis courts after 0.1 miles.
- Follow Stetson Rd. to Eph's pond and the playing fields (1.0 mi. total).
- Park to the left, along the barrier. Please do not block the gate or roadway.

DESCRIPTION

The open playing fields of Cole Field allow a 360-degree view of **Pine Cobble** to the east, the **Greylock Range** to the south, the **Taconic Range** to the west, and the **Dome** to the north. Hiking trails lace all of these areas and descriptions follow in later chapters. Refer to the map provided with this book to aid identification of these areas.

Eph's pond is part of a very altered floodplain area. Nevertheless, wildlife abounds, including over 100 species of birds, numerous amphibians, mammals, and reptiles. Refer to *A Guide to Natural Places in the Berkshire Hills* (see bibliography) for more information about the flora and fauna of Eph's Pond and the **Hoosic River**.

A warm spring or summer evening is the perfect time to listen to peepers while walking along the edge of Eph's Pond or continue on to the Hoosic River. Also, one can sight migratory waterfowl in the spring and autumn.

WILLIAMS COLLEGE RIVERWALK

Distance: Less than one mile
Estimated time: 30 – 60 minutes
Blazes: None
Map location: I – 20
Maintenance: Hoosic River Watershed Association

Williamstown lies at the confluence of the Green and Hoosic Rivers. Centuries ago, these waterways were the focus of life as sources of water and food, and as a means of transportation. Later, water powered the early industrial revolution, yet many New England towns turned their backs on local waterways, using them as sewers and dumping grounds, channeling the riverbeds, and developing land up to the rivers' edge. Not until the Clean Water Act in 1972 and new ethics of watershed management did towns begin to clean formerly life-giving waterways. However, even today, the Green and Hoosic Rivers are hidden behind buildings with few access points or trails. Cole Field provides excellent access to the Hoosic within the North Adams–Williamstown corridor.

HOW TO GET THERE
 • Refer to directions for Eph's Pond (page 35).

DESCRIPTION

From Eph's Pond, walk north, around a gate and along a paved path towards the Hoosic River and floodplain forest. As the blacktop path bears right toward a softball field and canoe launch, look for a wide gravel path to the left. The woods here are young, grown since a landfill on this site closed in 1972. This area has been severely impacted, yet offers a close look at the Hoosic River and riparian habitat.

Follow the footpath to a T-intersection with a sign indicating a right turn to "Sandy Beach" and a left turn for "Syndicate Road." Sandy Beach lies about 100 feet down a narrow footpath and offers a peaceful, shaded access point to the Hoosic.

As you continue towards Syndicate Road, notice the riprap, concrete blocks and rock lining the banks to prevent erosion and meandering of the river. The Hoosic drains all of north Berkshire and flows northwest to join the Hudson River in New York. During high water, sections of the trail you walk on lie underwater, and at flood stage the playing fields may be inundated as well!

After about 100 yards, the trail splits again. The right path leads to Syndicate Road, and a left turn will bring you back to a grassy path near Cole Field's golf driving range and Eph's Pond.

The right path to Syndicate Road brings you along the river's edge, and in about 0.1 mi., you arrive at yet another fork in the trail. Here, a right turn leads to Gravel Beach. A left takes you to Syndicate Road.

The path to Gravel Beach emerges into a secluded spot at a gentle bend in the river. The towering cottonwoods on the far bank shield this area from sight: except for the sounds of distant car traffic, you could be in the middle of nowhere!

From here, return along the path to the previous intersection. You can retrace your steps to the trailhead, or take the path to Syndicate Road. After a short distance, cross a small footbridge before entering a clear, grassy area. Ahead is Syndicate Road. To return to your car, follow the grassy right-of-way to the left. A footpath shares the byway with a sewer line to the Williamstown Sewage Treatment Plant, located across the Hoosic River to the north.

Note: Due to concerted efforts in recent decades, the Hoosic River is classified as suitable for swimming and fishing, but eating fish caught below North Adams (and its industrial sites) is not recommended. Take care and do not drink from the river!

HOOSIC RIVER NATURE TRAIL

Distance: Less than 0.5 mile
Estimated time: 20 minutes
Map location: J – 19
Blazes: None
Maintenance: Williamstown Rural Lands Foundation and Hoosic River Watershed Association

This short walking trail begins in the historic Mill Village neighborhood of Williamstown, and leads through riparian habitat as you walk along the Hoosic and Green Rivers.

HOW TO GET THERE

From campus or Spring Street, an on-foot approach can make this into a pleasant 2-hour walk through town.

- Drive east on Route 2 to the first stop light (0.6 mi.).
- Turn left on Cole Avenue and drive north toward the Hoosic River.
- Before the river, turn right on Arnold St. (1.1 mi.).
- Immediately turn left on Mill Street (one way).
- Follow Mill Street to a sign marking the Nature Trail (1.3 mi.). Park off the road.

DESCRIPTION

Local efforts to improve Hoosic River access led to this trail on Williamstown land. From the end of Mill Street, walk east down to the Hoosic River floodplain. A footpath follows the right-of-way of the municipal sewer line upstream to the Green River confluence.

You may wander up the Green River towards Route 2, or loop back to Mill Street along the riverside nature trail.

LEHOVEC RIVER WALK
Distances: 0.5 miles
Estimated time: 20 minutes
Map location: J – 19
   (Note: trail not marked on map as of 2019 printing)
Blazes: None
Maintenance: Williamstown Rural Lands Foundation

Like the nearby Hoosic River Nature Trail, this short walk leads through riparian habitat as you make your way along the Green River.

HOW TO GET THERE
From campus or Spring Street, an on-foot approach can make this into a pleasant 2-hour walk through town.
   • Drive east on Route 2 to the first stop light (0.6 mi.).
   • Turn left on Cole Avenue and drive north toward the Hoosic River.
   • Turn right on Saulnier Dr. (0.9 mi.).
   • Continue on Saulnier as it bears right and becomes Wood-lawn Dr.
   • Follow Woodlawn to its terminus and park off the road. (1.0 mi.).

DESCRIPTION
From the cul-de-sac (0.0 mi.) walk down a short, moderate hill to a broad, grassy path: a municipal right-of-way for the town sewer. Turn left (east), and walk along the river. After 0.1 mi., the path bears left, away from the river's edge. After another 100 yards, you will see a trail on your right leading into the woods. It is marked by a sign indicating the start of the Lehovec River Walk.

As you make your way towards the river, you pass through riparian habitat. Note the tall ostrich ferns (shaped like the tailfeathers of their namesake!), and overhead the towering cottonwood, locust, and willow trees. At the riverbank (0.3 mi.), turn left, walking downstream alongside the current before heading away and up a short, steep rise built from large rock slabs: rip-rap, placed here to help hold the bank in place. Just beyond, you arrive back at the town right-of-way. A left turn takes you past the Lehovec River

Walk trailhead and back to your car (0.5 mi.). A right turn leads eventually to the **Hoosic River Nature Trail**.

LINEAR PARK
Distance: Short walk
Estimated time: 30 minutes or more
Blazes: Some faded blue
Map location: I– 18
Maintenance: Town of Williamstown

This small park, maintained by the town of Williamstown, is a convenient place to eat a picnic lunch or spend a quiet hour enjoying the outdoors. The Green River, flowing to the Hoosic River, passes through the park.

HOW TO GET THERE
Linear Park may be reached on foot from Spring Street or any location on the Williams Campus via a number of different routes. If you are visiting the park for the first time, or you are in a car, use the following directions.
- Take Route 2 east to Water Street (Route 43).
- Turn right on Water Street, and follow it 0.2 mi. to a bridge over the Green River on the left.
- You will see a sign for the park as you cross the bridge.
- Around the bend to the right is a small gravel parking area with room for 3-4 cars.

DESCRIPTION
At first glance, Linear Park is a grassy area with several picnic tables, two barbecue grills, and a variety of play equipment for children. A short scramble down the slope behind the picnic tables to the Green River brings you to a different world: the noise of flowing water quiets the cars and trucks above, and the cleft of the riverway obscures buildings and pavement. An old path along the river marked with blue blazes connects gravel bars and sculpted phyllite outcrops. Explore and find your own spot to read, study, or watch the water flow by.

The Green River is generally considered to be suitable for fishing and swimming. Agricultural activity upstream may introduce bacteria to the water. Avoid ingesting the water, but cooling off on a hot summer day is safe thanks to local conservation efforts. Contact the Hoosic River Watershed Association if you have concerns about water quality.

LINEAR PARK NORTH

Distance: Short walk
Estimated time: 30 minutes or more
Blazes: Blue
Map location: J– 19
Maintenance: Town of Williamstown, Williamstown Rural Lands Foundation

This park is a situated at the confluence of the Green River and Hoosic River. It includes tennis courts and trails.

HOW TO GET THERE

By car or foot.
- Take Route 2 east, past the Cole Ave. intersection.
- Turn left at Linear Park road (1.0 mi), after passing the cemetary to your right.

DESCRIPTION

Park next to the tennis courts. The trails begin along a road, to the right of a sign board with a map and information about the area. A trail to the southeast skirts an old corn field. Explore vibrant flood-plain forest to the northwest.

A town sewer line passes through this park. Follow it to the edge of the Green River, cross if you can, and you'll find yourself on the **Hoosic River Nature Trail**, described earlier in this section.

BURBANK TRAIL

Distance: 0.8 mile
Estimated time: 40 minutes
Map location: J – 17
Blazes: Various (yellow, blue, pink)
Maintenance: Williamstown Conservation Commission

This short walking trail follows the edge of farm fields and affords stunning views of Mt. Prospect, Pine Cobble, and the Taconics.

HOW TO GET THERE

- From the intersection of Rts. 2 and 7 in Williamstown, follow Route 2 east.
- Turn right on Adams Road (1.2 mi.).
- Turn right on Stratton Road (1.3 mi.).
- Continue until the pavement turns to gravel and park on the right (2.2 mi.).

DESCRIPTION

The trailhead for the Burbank Trail begins on the left (east) side of the road at the edge of a large field (0.0 mi.). Walk across the field to the far hedgerow (0.25 mi.), and turn right (south), following the tree line. Keep the trees on your left. Take a 90-degree left turn (east) between an opening in the hedgerow, and after ten yards exit to a small stretch of grass. At the southeast corner (ahead and to the right) of this small field, the trail enters the woods on a double-track trail (0.35 mi.). The trail eventually crosses a seasonal stream bed before bringing you to another small field. Cross it, and head through the far hedgerow, which brings you to a much larger field. Walk left (north) and follow the tree line on your left as it eventually turns 90-degrees east and then again, to the south (0.7 mi.). Look for an opening in the hedgerow soon after this last turn, on your left. Head downhill on a meandering woods footpath. At the path's low-point, cross a small stream and then hike uphill to exit at Luce Road (0.8 mi.). Walk back to the trailhead through the neighborhoods, or retrace your steps.

OTHER WALKS IN WILLIAMSTOWN

You do not need a guidebook to explore the streets of Williamstown. Any time of year you can set out for a stroll along the centuries-old roads, many of which follow original footpaths. If you like to run, check out *A Runner's Guide to Williamstown*, available in local bookstores. Below are a few suggested routes, listed from shortest to longer. Use the map provided with this book - or a Williamstown map - to find your way.

Stetson Road to Cole Field to Cole Avenue.
West Main Street to Northwest Hill Road to Bulkley Street.
South Street to Gale or Ide Road.
Route 43 to Blair Road to Stratton Road.

STONE HILL

Early settlers named Stone Hill for the outcroppings of quartzite that were visible along the ridge when most trees had been cleared from the hill in the 18th century. Geologists speculate that these rocks, now obscured by vegetation, are the solidified and meta-morphosed remains of a sandy ocean coastline from about 550 million years ago, formed while the majority of this region was in the tropical latitudes. Since the rock tends to be quite intensely fractured, settlers often used it for building.

Stone Hill is one of the most popular places to walk and hike in the Williamstown area. There are a number of trails that may be combined to form loops of different lengths and difficulty. Described here are the Nan Path, Howard Path, Woodland Trail, Hopkins-Gale Trail, Pasture Trail, Stone Bench Trail, Stone Hill Road Trail, Buxton School Trail, Carl Reidel Trail, Kite Hill Trail, and the Pine Cobble School Trail, in that order. A detailed map is available at ClarkArt.edu. The Town of Williamstown, The Sterling and Francine Clark Art Institute, Williams College, and several private landholders own and manage the land over which trails pass. Although Stone Hill has long been open to public wandering, please respect postings and private property.

Stone Bench–Found on top of Stone Hill.
Drawing by Mark Livingston '72.

NAN PATH

Distance: 0.4 miles
Estimated time: 20 minutes
Blazes: Royal blue
Map location: H – 18
Maintenance: Clark Art Institute

This peaceful walk takes you along a meandering gravel path through the woods from the main Clark Art campus to the Lunder Center, and provides access to other trails along the way.

HOW TO GET THERE

- From the intersection of Routes 2 and 7, head south on South Street (opposite Route 7 north).
- After 0.5 mi., turn right at The Clark Art Institute's campus.
- If you are driving, follow the road to the north side of the museum buildings and park in one of the lots.
- Continue to the backside of the Manton Research Building (the red granite building) and head towards the footbridge near the building's south side.
- The trailhead is marked by a small informational placard and two small gravestones at the forest's edge.

DESCRIPTION

The two small gravestones (0.0 mi.) mark the burial place of dogs that belonged to an earlier property owner, Dr. Vanderpool Adriance. The trail begins on the right and takes you across a long footbridge, the first of many. After the bridge, the packed gravel path winds uphill through a variety of birch, beech, and maple stands, as well as some oak, hemlock, and pine. At 0.25 mi. a signed trail junction marks the turn-off for the **Woodland Trail** to the right. The Woodland Trail allows access to the **Pasture Trail**, **Stone Hill Road Trail**, **Hopkins-Gale Trail**, **Stone Bench Trail**, **Carl Reidel Trail**, and the **Buxton School Trail**. Continue straight past the Woodland Trail turnoff and soon arrive at another junction (0.3 mi.), where continuing straight would lead you to the Pasture Trail and Stone Bench Trail. Turn left and cross the long bridge to join the **Howard Path** before arriving at the Lunder Center. The Nan Path is wheelchair accessible, dependent on weather.

HOWARD PATH
Distance: 0.25 miles
Estimated time: 15 minutes
Blazes: Navy blue
Map location: H – 18
Maintenance: Clark Art Institute

This short, paved trail provides the most direct footpath from the main Clark Art campus to the Lunder Center.

HOW TO GET THERE
- Refer to directions for the Nan Path (page 45).

DESCRIPTION
Begin at the placard and gravestones as for the **Nan Path**, and walk across the bridge. After crossing, turn left onto the paved trail. This is the beginning of the Howard Path (0.0 mi.). Soon after you start, the path begins winding through the woods and you pass a turnoff on the right for the **Woodland Trail**. Continue straight and make your way over a long wooden walkway. You may notice here that the trail parallels the road to the Lunder Center. As you approach the Center, a bench marks a spot to sit and enjoy the woods (0.3 mi.). Depending on your destination, you can exit the woods here to visit the Lunder Center, or continue on across a long wooden bridge. At its end is a T-junction. Turn left to access the **Pasture Trail** and **Stone Bench Trail**, or turn right onto the Nan Path to return to the trailhead where you began your walk. The Howard Path has steps and therefore is not wheelchair accessible.

WOODLAND TRAIL
Distance: 0.3 miles
Estimated time: 15 minutes
Blazes: Green
Map location: H - 18
Maintenance: Clark Art Institute

This short, rugged trail winds through the woods before depositing you at the Stone Hill Road Trail.

HOW TO GET THERE
- Refer to directions for the Nan Path (page 45).

DESCRIPTION

Begin at the placard and gravestones as for the **Nan Path**, and take an immediate left to the **Howard Path**. Walk for about 100 yards to reach the start of the Woodland Trail (0.0 mi.), on the right (west).

In this damp, shrubby part of the forest, you might notice the pervasive invasive species winged euonymus, also known commonly as 'burning bush' for its fiery red leaves during autumn. Take a closer look and you will see the fine 'wings' on its stem.

Continue walking on this single-track trail and pass straight through the intersection with the Nan Path at 0.1 mi. From here, the trail widens as you wind uphill to another four-way intersection (0.25 mi.). A right turn takes you along the **Pasture Trail**, and a left leads to the Lunder Center. Walk straight through to complete the Woodland Trail: its terminus is marked by the **Stone Hill Road Trail**, directly across from the **Hopkins-Gale Trail** (0.4 mi.).

HOPKINS-GALE TRAIL

Distance: 1.0 mile
Estimated time: 40 minutes
Blazes: Orange
Map location: G - 18
Maintenance: Buxton School, Williams College, Williamstown Conservation Commission

This winding path parallels the Stone Hill Road Trail, taking you deep into the forest near Stone Hill's summit.

HOW TO GET THERE
- Refer to directions for the Nan Path (page 45).

DESCRIPTION

Begin at the trail sign and gravestones as for the **Nan Path**, and make your way to the **Woodland Trail** by following this path, or by choosing the **Howard Path**. Follow the Woodland Trail to its terminus at a wide gravel road, the junction with the **Stone Hill Road Trail**. Across this road is the start of the Hopkins-Gale Trail (0.0 mi.). You can also access this point via the **Stone Hill Road** Trail 0.2 mi. uphill from the Lunder Center parking lot.

Hike uphill to start, following orange blazes as you walk through oak and beech trees. At 0.2 mi., arrive at a junction. On your right (west) is one end of the **Stone Bench Trail**. One-hundred yards beyond is the Stone Bench. The Hopkins-Gale Trail continues straight ahead.

Here is perhaps the most pleasant path on Stone Hill: wide, smooth, sinuous and rolling, with hemlock groves and intermittent phyllite outcrops. In winter, look to the west and north through bare trees for a fantastic view of the Taconic Range. Note the trailhead for the **Carl Reidel Trail** (white blazes) on your left (east) at 0.4 mi., near a particularly rocky outcropping. A little farther uphill, a lone hemlock marks a spot to sit, reflect, and enjoy the view (0.5 mi.). Just beyond that is a sign marking the highest point of Stone Hill: 1,145'.

At a stone wall that once delineated the boundary between two fields (0.6 mi.), a junction with the **Buxton School Trail** leads left (east), without crossing the wall. Jog right and then continue straight through the stone wall, following the orange blazes, to reach the terminus of the Hopkins-Gale Trail where it meets the **Kite Hill Trail**. A right turn here takes you along the Kite Hill Trail to the Stone Hill Road Trail, and a left follows all the way to Kite Hill and Cluett Drive.

PASTURE TRAIL

Distances: 0.7 miles
Estimated time: 30 minutes
Blazes: Pinkish-red
Map location: H – 18
Maintenance: Clark Art Institute

A wonderful walk to, and through, the pasture above The Clark. Students and townspeople alike return again and again to enjoy the spectacular view of Williamstown, Pine Cobble, and the Dome to the north.

HOW TO GET THERE
- Refer to directions for the Nan Path (page 45).

DESCRIPTION

Begin at the trail sign and gravestones as for the **Nan Path**, and make your way along this gravel path for 0.3 mi. to the signed trail junction marking the turn-off for the Lunder Center to the left (east). Continue straight to begin the Pasture Trail (0.0 mi.).

The Pasture Trail soon intersects the **Woodland Path** (0.1 mi.). Continue straight and make your way to a gate at the edge of the field. After passing through, be sure to close it behind you. A worn path leads west across the pasture to a grove of trees with excellent views (0.5 mi.). Grazing cows often dot the pasture and may glance at you, but pose no threat to your safety. To return to The Clark below, follow the double track downhill on the far side of the field, straight to a gate in the fence that eventually brings you to the Clark Art Institute's main parking lot (0.7 mi.). Again, please close the gate behind you.

Many people choose to walk this trail in reverse. To do so, start at the Clark Art Institute's main parking lot and head 0.5 mi. southerly uphill to the top of the rise. Then, hike left 0.2 mi. across the meadow and into the woods. Continue downhill on the Nan Path to the Clark Art Institute buildings.

STONE BENCH TRAIL

Distances: 0.9 miles
Estimated time: 35 minutes
Blazes: Black
Map location: H – 18
Maintenance: Clark Art Institute

For a slightly longer walk than the Pasture Loop, try a trip up to the Stone Bench. The bench is dedicated to George Moritz Wahl, a former professor of German at Williams College who climbed to this spot every evening to watch the sunset. During World War I he was subjected to substantial abuse because of his ethnic background, but when he died shortly after the war, his students and fellow townspeople erected the bench as a memorial and symbol of their regret. Although trees now obscure the view of the Taconic Range to the west, the bench is a pleasant place for a quiet moment of reflection.

HOW TO GET THERE
• Refer to directions for the Nan Path (page 45).

DESCRIPTION
Begin at the trail sign and gravestones as for the **Nan Path**, and continue on this gravel trail for 0.3 mi. to the signed intersection with the **Woodland Path**. Turn right onto the Woodland Path and continue for another 0.2 mi. straight through its intersection with the **Pasture Trail** until you arrive at a broad gravel path, the **Stone Hill Road Trail**. Across this path is the start of the **Hopkins-Gale Trail**. After 0.2 mi. on this trail, you will see the turnoff for the Stone Bench Trail on your right (0.0 mi.). This is the beginning of the trail.

Head up and over the small rise (notice the phyllite outcropping on the right) to arrive at the Stone Bench. This spot marks another intersection with the Stone Hill Road Trail. To continue your hike, continue straight (west) past the bench and across a small clearing. Follow the trail as it curves gently north. Pass through a small hemlock grove interspersed with oaks. Mind your footing here: the path narrows and there are many exposed roots. Exit through a gate into the brilliant view of the pasture overlooking Williamstown (0.4 mi.). Please remember to close the gate behind you.

Walk downhill through the pasture, and make your way to the small grove of trees with one of the best views of town (0.7 mi.). Here, you can see much of the Clark Art Institute's campus, as well as **Williamstown** and the **Green Mountains** beyond. Follow the gravel path downhill towards the Clark Art Institute, as the Stone Bench Trail briefly joins the Pasture Trail for 0.1 mi. Keep an eye out for the turnoff (0.75 mi.) where the Stone Bench Trail branches to the right (east). This trail cuts diagonally downhill before depositing you at a small gate in the fence (0.8 mi.). Cross through onto the Nan Path, and turn left. Again, please remember to close the gate behind you. Follow the bridge and return to the trailhead where you began your hike.

STONE HILL ROAD TRAIL

Distance: 2.0 mile
Estimated time: 50 minutes (one way)
Blazes: Red
Map location: H - 18
Maintenance: Buxton School, Clark Art Institute, Williams College, Williamstown Conservation Commission

This, after all, was the prime North-South road in New England [connecting Pittsfield, MA to Bennington, VT]. Over this road went soldiers to Bennington in 1777; President Washington, riding over the hill in 1790, paused at this spot to take in what was then an open view of the fledgling town, with its new Free School; and every day townsfolk trafficked the road between North and South villages. To the struggling college this was the slender umbilicus of an indifferent world.

- Arthur Latham Perry

The Stone Hill Road Trail is the main artery off of which many Stone Hill trails branch. This former roadway offers access to the northern termini of the Carl Reidel Trail, Hopkins-Gale Trail, and the Buxton School Trail, and the western terminus of the Kite Hill Trail. It also crosses paths with the Stone Bench and Woodland Trails.

HOW TO GET THERE

- From the intersection of Routes 2 and 7, head south on South Street (opposite Route 7 north).
- After 0.5 mi., turn right into the second of The Clark's two driveways.
- Follow the road as it curves and park in the first small parking lot on your left.
- Walk east to South Street, and turn right to head towards Buxton School as South Street becomes Gale Road and bears left.
- After 100 yards, there is a gated gravel road on your right.

DESCRIPTION

From the metal gate (0.0 mi.), hike up gravel road. At the top of the rise, the **Buxton School Trail** begins on the left (just past the Lunder Center on the right). Continue uphill past the start of the **Carl Reidel Trail**, also on the left. As you make your way on this broad path, pass through the four-way intersection with the **Woodland Path Trail** (right; north) and the **Hopkins-Gale Trail** (left; south) before reaching a field under which the Williamstown water tank lies buried.

Gravel gives way to mulch and dirt that lead to the **Stone Bench** on the left (0.7 mi.). From here, Stone Hill Road continues to the south, just below and to the west of Stone Hill's spine. You will pass a number of quartzite outcrops on the left. At approximately 1.25 mi. the **Kite Hill Trail** heads east while Stone Hill Road Trail continues south. A number of fields border the road and offer fine views east and west.

At about 2.0 mi., Stone Hill Road Trail becomes a maintained town road and continues to Scott Hill Road (2.5 mi.). From here you will want to return along the same route or be picked up; otherwise, you face a long return trip on Route 7 or Route 43. Be careful if you choose to return northward on one of these busy highways.

BUXTON SCHOOL TRAIL

Distances: 0.9 miles
Estimated time: 40 minutes
Blazes: Forest green with white outline
Map location: H – 18
Maintenance: Buxton School

This path takes advantage of old forest roads as it makes its way up the eastern flank of Stone Hill. Pay close attention as you hike: there are many abandoned, partially grown-in logging roads crisscrossing the main trail. A small side-loop brings hikers near the Buxton School before returning again to the main Buxton School Trail.

HOW TO GET THERE

- From the intersection of Routes 2 and 7, head south on South Street (opposite Route 7 north).
- After 0.5 mi., turn right into the second of The Clark's two driveways.
- Follow the driveway 0.5 mi. as it winds and then heads uphill.
- Park in the Lunder Center's parking lot.
- To find the trailhead: when facing the front of the Lunder Center, turn right and walk 100 yards to the east (crossing the Stone Hill Road Trail at the sign post with both red and green signs).
- Walk another 30 feet, and the Buxton School Trail begins on your right.

DESCRIPTION

Head into the forest and make your way across more than 20 small footbridges. Note the exposed tree roots – a symptom of water constantly draining through – and watch your step!

At 0.1 mi., a small side-loop begins on the left (east) and provides access to Buxton School if you're interested, or simply a longer hike. If you intend to use the side-loop only to make your hike longer, ignore the small spurs exiting into Buxton School's open fields, and continue straight on the trail for 0.4 mi. before arriving back to the main Buxton School Trail.

Continue past the side-loop to stay on the main Buxton School Trail. At 0.3 mi., the side-loop rejoins on the left (southeast) and you begin making your way uphill with real purpose. Notice the deep side-cut into the hill on your right, a sign of the trail's former use as a road. To make the grade wide and flat, part of the hill needed excavation. The path winds through broad switchbacks at 0.7 mi. and 0.8 mi., and tree cover diminishes as you near Stone Hill's high point. A final turn takes you due west, and you come upon an intricate stone wall. Keep it on your left as you reach the Buxton School Trail's end, where it meets a T-intersection with the **Hopkins-Gale Trail**. Return the way you came, or turn left (south) to access the **Kite Hill Trail** and **Stone Hill Road Trail**. A right turn (north) takes you along the Hopkins-Gale Trail to its start on the **Stone Hill Road Trail**, passing the terminus of the **Carl Reidel Trail** along the way.

CARL REIDEL TRAIL

Distances: 0.5 miles
Estimated time: 20 minutes
Blazes: White
Map location: H – 18
Maintenance: Williamstown Conservation Commission

This rambling single-track trail takes you deep into the Stone Hill woods, and brings you to a midway point on the Hopkins-Gale Trail. At the Reidel Trail's end, you can 'choose your own adventure' and combine it with any number of trails for a short jaunt or a longer hike of your choosing.

HOW TO GET THERE
- Refer to directions for the Nan Path (page 45).

DESCRIPTION

From the **Nan Path** trailhead, make your way on foot to South Street using the Clark Art Institute's main entrance. Turn right and head towards the road to the Buxton School as South Street becomes Gale Road and bears left. After 100 yards, there is a gated gravel road on your right. Hike uphill, and at the top of the rise, you will see the **Buxton School Trail** beginning on the left (just past the Lunder Center on the right). Continue uphill to the start of the Carl Reidel Trail, also on the left. The trailhead is marked by a kiosk with a trail map. Yellow "Town of Williamstown" boundary markers are posted on nearby trees.

Enter the woods here (0.0 mi.) and wind uphill for 0.1 mi. The trail levels before dropping into a hemlock forest, and not long after, it crosses a small rivulet at the trail's low point. Make your way uphill again. At 0.3, exit the hemlocks into deciduous oak and beech forest. For much of this hike, you have been winding your way around the periphery of Stone Hill's peak, but now you hike straight uphill through the most rugged part of the trail (0.4 mi.).

At 0.5 mi. arrive at a T-junction with the **Hopkins-Gale Trail** running north-to-south. Many people choose to take a right (north) and follow the Hopkins-Gale Trail 0.5 mi. back to its start at the **Stone Hill Road Trail** before taking another right to return to the Clark Art Institute.

KITE HILL TRAIL
Distances: 1.0 mile
Estimated time: 40 minutes
Blazes: Yellow
Map location: I – 17
Maintenance: Williams College

In 1994, the Williams Outing Club and townspeople cut two trails on Williams College-owned property – the Kite Hill Trail and the Pine Cobble School Trail – to connect the Stone Hill Road Trail to Pine Cobble School and Gale Road.

HOW TO GET THERE
- From the intersection of Routes 2 and 7, go south on South Street (opposite Route 7 north)
- Continue on South Street as it bears left and becomes Gale Road (0.5 mi.)
- Turn right on Cluett Drive and park at the end of the cul-de-sac (1.4 mi.)

DESCRIPTION
From the parking area, walk a short distance along one of two mowed paths against the sweeping backdrop of Mts. Prospect and Greylock. Turn right (west) and head towards the selvedge. At 0.3 mi., the turnoff for the **Pine Cobble School Trail** branches to the right (north), while the Kite Hill Trail continues in the opposite direction and takes you along a straightaway with branches arcing overhead. After 0.4 mi., reach a T-intersection: the Kite Hill trail takes a 90-degree right turn (west) into the forest. A left turn allows you to continue on the mowed grass path, touring the field where you began your hike.

The Kite Hill Trail leads downhill across a seasonal stream before bringing you to higher ground. Hook a right past the metal fence and post, signs of the land's former use, and continue across a flat stretch before hiking generally downhill. Cross another small seasonal stream and begin a sustained climb uphill.

At 0.3 mi., the trail becomes particularly root-y and rocky – runoff has eroded the soil, and small footbridges lead the way. Continue uphill. Note the massive phyllite formation rising from the forest floor on your left (0.5 mi). Make your way uphill past this rock formation. There is another one, this time on your right, at 0.7 mi. Look how the oak tree has spread its roots across the entirety of the rock, front-to-back!

Keep an eye out for the **Hopkins-Gale Trail**, which meets the Kite Hill Trail at 0.9 mi. Continue past this junction and arrive at **Stone Hill Road Trail** (1.0 mi.). Return the way you came, or try a combination of other trails for a longer hike.

PINE COBBLE SCHOOL TRAIL

Distances: 0.5 miles
Estimated time: 20 minutes
Blazes: Lime green
Map location: I – 17
Maintenance: Williams College

The Pine Cobble School Trail is one of two trails (the other is the Kite Hill Trail) cut in 1994 by the Williams Outing Club and townspeople that connects Pine Cobble School and Gale Road to the Stone Hill Road Trail.

HOW TO GET THERE
• Refer to directions for the Kite Hill Trail (page 55).

DESCRIPTION
From the parking area, walk a short distance along one of two mowed paths against the sweeping backdrop of Mts. Prospect and Greylock. Turn right (west) and head towards the selvedge. At 0.3 mi., arrive at the turnoff (0.0 mi.) for the Pine Cobble School Trail on your right (north). The **Kite Hill Trail** continues in the opposite direction.

Begin hiking on the Pine Cobble School Trail, downhill through a thicket of buckthorn and winged euonymus. The shrubs soon give way to an open meadow. The land here has been shaped by the presence of beavers, and at 0.25 mi. you pass a vernal pool. In the spring, this is the breeding site of wood frogs! After passing the pond, reenter the thicket and make sure to respect the "private property" sign at 0.4 mi., where another trail splits away to the left. Continue right, and arrive at the trail's end at Gale Road (0.5 mi.). Return the way you came, or turn right (southeast) to stay on the road a short distance until reaching Cluett Drive, where you began.

GREEN MOUNTAINS

The Green Mountains Section includes the region north of the Hoosic River. Although several of these trails are in Vermont, they are described in this guide because the Dome and East Mountain effectively form a northern physiographic boundary of the North Berkshire area.

These mountains are the southern extremities of the Green Mountains, a range that extends several hundred miles north into Vermont. Although more than 400-million years old, the Green Mountains remain quite rugged, with sharp crests and steep slopes. The average elevation of the ridgeline today is 2,000 feet, with several peaks rising to heights of 4,000 feet or more. The lower slopes are covered with northern hardwoods, while above 3,000 feet are the evergreen forests for which the range was named.

Recreational use of the Green Mountains began over 100 years ago with the construction of "summit houses," rustic hotels where vacationers could spend a few weeks enjoying the mountain scenery. The Green Mountain Club (GMC) was founded in 1910, and shortly afterward began construction of the Long Trail. This "footpath in the wilderness" now extends the length of Vermont, from the Massachusetts/Vermont line to the Canadian border, for a total of 265 miles. Pine Cobble trails serve as a southern gateway to the state border and Long Trail.

The GMC maintains over seventy primitive shelters and many tenting areas a moderate day's journey apart over the entire length of the trail. The southern 136 miles of the Long Trail also forms a link of the Appalachian Trail, a 2,190 mile (approximately) trail that extends the length of the Appalachian Mountains from Maine to Georgia.

PINE COBBLE TRAIL

Distances: 1.6 miles to Pine Cobble, 2.1 miles to Appalachian Trail

Estimated time: 1 hour to Pine Cobble

Blazes: Blue

Map location: J – 19

Maintenance: Williams Outing Club

Pine Cobble (1,894 feet), to the northeast of Williamstown, offers one of the finest panoramic views of the Hoosic River valley. Within easy walking distance of the Williams College campus, this hike is a favorite with many Williams College students. The word "cobble" refers to the exposed outcropping of quartzite bedrock that is the destination of most of those who use the trail. On a clear day, the outcrop is easily visible from the valley floor, several miles away.

HOW TO GET THERE

If on foot, head north across the Williams campus. Pass the tennis courts and walk down Stetson Rd. to Cole Field. Follow the road around Eph's Pond, east through a gate to Cole Avenue. Turn left, cross the Hoosic River to the intersection with North Hoosac Rd. Diagonally right across North Hoosac Rd., Cole's Grove Rd. leads around a gate and into the Pine Cobble Development. At the mailboxes, turn right. The trailhead is 300 yards down the road on the left. By car:

- Take Route 2 east from its junction with Route 7.
- After 0.6 mi., turn left on Cole Ave. at the first stoplight.
- You will cross a bridge over the Hoosic River and railroad tracks just before North Hoosac Rd.
- Turn right on N. Hoosac (1.4 mi.) and then left on Pine Cobble Road at 1.8 miles.
- Park in the parking area on the left, 0.2 mi. up the hill. The trailhead is across the road.

DESCRIPTION

At the Pine Cobble Trail sign (0.0 mi.), hike parallel to the road for 200 yards before turning left and ascending gradually into the woods. The trail levels out on a plateau (0.5 mi.), once the shore of glacial Lake Bascom, which filled the entire Hoosac Valley to a depth of about 500 feet!

A side trail to the right marks the halfway point (0.8 mi.). It leads 350 feet downhill to **Bear Spring**, a slight upwelling at the base of a steep cliff topped with hemlocks. Since the spring is the only open water on the south side of Pine Cobble, it attracts many species of wildlife, including chipmunks, rabbits, and deer.

Continue at a moderately steep grade, past the beginning of the **Class of '98 Trail**, to a more level area at 1.0 mi. where the trail turns to the southeast. Yellow diamond-shaped tags mark the boundary of the WRLF Pine Cobble Summit Natural Area. Cross two small jumbled rock outcroppings and follow a sharp left turn at the intersection with an old trail (1.1 mi.).

Watch for an unusual triplet oak tree with a water-filled basin at its center (1.4 mi.). After the original tree was cut down, three shoots sprouted around the edges of the old stump while the center rotted away. This flat section of the trail is also an excellent place to see trailing arbutus, the Massachusetts state flower, which usually blooms in early April.

A steep stretch completes the climb (1.5 mi.). From the trail sign at the crest of the hill, several short (0.1 mi.) trails to the right lead out onto the quartzite outcrops of Pine Cobble. Enjoy an excellent view of the **Greylock Range** across the valley to the south, with the summit of Mt. Greylock clearly distinguished by the war memorial and communications towers. The **Taconic Range** forms the western horizon, while the top of the **Dome** is visible to the north. Looking down into the **Hoosic River** valley, North Adams is to the east and Williamstown to the southwest.

Proceeding left (north) from the trail sign, you pass an anchor point for an old utility pole and emerge onto a boulder field. A short climb leads to the summit of East Mountain, where the Pine Cobble Trail joins the **Appalachian Trail** (2.1 mi.). This is the site of an old forest fire, now covered with blueberry bushes, and it provides limited views of the Taconic and Greylock Ranges.

CLASS OF '98 TRAIL
Distance: 1.5 miles, Pine Cobble Trail to Appalachian Trail
Estimated time: 1 hour to Appalachian Trail
Blazes: Blue
Map location: K - 19
Maintenance: Williams Outing Club

The '98 Trail, completed by Williams students in 1999, was designed by Chris Elkington '98 as a gift from his class to the College. Together, the '98, Appalachian, and Pine Cobble Trails form a 2.5 mi. circuit, with interesting rock outcrops and panoramic views.

HOW TO GET THERE
- From the Pine Cobble Trail: Follow the Pine Cobble Trail for 0.9 mi. from its trailhead. The junction with the '98 trail, marked with blue blazes, is on the left, opposite a sign indicating 0.8 mi. remain to Pine Cobble.

DESCRIPTION
The first leg of the trail heads north from the **Pine Cobble Trail** and follows a flat grade along the base of one of the area's characteristic quartzite outcrops, with views of boulders and small cliffs. Note the many pairs and triplets of oak trees, the result of sprouts coming off stumps left by logging. The biggest cliffs can be found just after passing the intersection with the **Chestnut Trail** (0.6 mi.).

Beyond the intersection, the trail passes through an area of dense regrowth forest and patches of mountain laurel (blooms in June), then begins the steep, rocky, ascent of the ridge it has been following (0.8 mi.). At 1.25 mi., the trail crosses the border of Clarksburg State Forest, which is also blazed with blue. After the first ascent, the trail climbs moderately to the intersection with the **Appalachian Trail** (1.5 mi.). Turn right (south) along the Appalachian Trail 0.2 mi. to the intersection with the Pine Cobble Trail.

CHESTNUT TRAIL

Distance: 0.7 miles
Estimated time: 30 minutes
Blazes: Blue
Map location: J - 20
Maintenance: Williamstown Rural Lands Foundation

In conjunction with the Class of '98 Trail, The Chestnut Trail offers an alternate route to Pine Cobble, from the Williamstown side.

HOW TO GET THERE

- Take Route 2 east from its junction with Route 7.
- After 0.6 mi., turn left on Cole Ave. at the first stoplight.
- You will cross a bridge over the Hoosic River and railroad tracks just before North Hoosac Rd.
- Turn left on N. Hoosac (1.4 mi.) and then right on Chestnut Street at 1.5 miles.
- The trailhead is on the right, opposite an open field, at about 1.7 mi. Park on the side of the road.

DESCRIPTION

From the sign at Chestnut Street, the trail follows an old forest road for a moderate 0.7 mi. climb through oak forest to the intersection with the **Class of '98 Trail**.

Sickly young American Chestnut trees may be found, sprouting from root systems established before the Chestnut Blight was introduced in the early 1900s. More common, however, is the Chestnut Oak.

At the intersection with the '98 Trail, turn right (south) for the most direct route to Pine Cobble, or take your pick to start a 2.5 mi. loop with the **Pine Cobble**, **Class of '98**, and **Appalachian Trails**.

PINE COBBLE VIA THE APPALACHIAN TRAIL

Distances: 2.5 miles to Pine Cobble Trail, 3.1 miles to Pine
Cobble
Estimated time: 1.5 hours
Blazes: White
Map location: M – 18
Maintenance: AMC Mass. AT Committee

For an alternate route up Pine Cobble from the Hoosac Valley, try this portion of the Appalachian Trail (AT) along Sherman Brook. Like the Pine Cobble Trail, it is also an approach trail to the Long Trail of Vermont, which officially starts at the Massachusetts-Vermont border. In mid-to-late summer you may meet a "thru-hiker" from Georgia following the Appalachian Trail to Mt. Katahdin in Maine.

HOW TO GET THERE

- Take Route 2 east from its junction with Route 7.
- After 0.6 mi., turn left on Cole Ave. at the first stoplight.
- You will cross a bridge over the Hoosic River and railroad tracks just before North Hoosac Rd.
- Turn right on N. Hoosac (1.4 mi.) and drive toward the historic Blackinton neighborhood (2.9 mi.). North Hoosac Rd. becomes Massachusetts Avenue in North Adams.
- You pass the AT Hoosic River footbridge to your right at 3.8 mi. Note white blazes on the telephone poles.
- After 0.1 mi. (3.9 mi. total) the AT crosses Massachusetts Ave. at Sherman Brook and heads north.
- Limited street parking is available at the trailhead.

DESCRIPTION

From Massachusetts Avenue (0.0 mi.), follow a narrow driveway north and cross two small footbridges before entering the woods (0.1 mi.). Follow the brook upstream for nearly a mile before making a short ascent out of the valley.

A blue-blazed side trail branches off to the left just beyond Pete's Spring (1.4 mi.), and continues 0.2 mi. through a camping area, with three tent platforms, an outhouse, and a ready supply of water from both Pete's Spring and Sherman Brook.

Looping below the campsite, the AT passes a confluence of Sherman Brook and follows a tributary to the northwest (1.6 mi.). Note old bridge abutments from a former wood road crossing. At 2.2 mi. you pass the first junction with the Bad Weather Bypass Trail, which avoids a difficult section of the main trail by looping to the southwest. Stop here to enjoy excellent views to the east.

From here, the AT swings to the west, climbing a steep, rocky slope with good views to the south and east (2.3 mi.). White and flesh-colored quartzite talus covers the bottom of each steep slope. The Bad Weather Trail rejoins the main trail at the top of this section. A marshy area (2.4 mi.) and a rocky knoll complete the ascent at the Pine Cobble Trail intersection (2.5 mi.).

APPALACHIAN TRAIL
PINE COBBLE TRAIL TO COUNTY ROAD

Distances: 4.5 miles to County Road
Estimated time: 2-3 hours
Blazes: White
Map location: L – 20
Maintenance: AMC Mass. AT Committee

This attractive, well-traveled section of the Appalachian Trail (AT) traverses the ridge of East Mountain to the Vermont State Line. There begins the 265-mile Long Trail to Canada (2.8 mi.). North of the border is a campsite and shelter named for Seth Warner, patriot and Green Mountain Boy in the American Revolution. You may use the AT to connect the Broad Brook and Pine Cobble Trails for a pleasant, 10.2 mile hike.

HOW TO GET THERE
   • Follow the Pine Cobble Trail 0.6 mi. past Pine Cobble or use the Appalachian Trail up Pine Cobble along Sherman Brook from Massachusetts Ave. in North Adams.

DESCRIPTION
From the **Pine Cobble Trail** and Appalachian Trail junction at East Mountain (0.0 mi.), proceed north across several quartzite outcrops. Soon after cresting one, pass the **Class of '98 Trail** to

the left (0.2 mi.). The largest of these exposed areas (0.5 mi.) is known as "Eph's Lookout" after Ephraim Williams, the founder of Williams College.

From here, the trail maintains a fairly level grade except for a short rise just before the Massachusetts-Vermont State Line (1.4 mi.). Here a trail register marks the official southern end of the **Long Trail** (LT). The AT/LT descends sharply on log and stone steps through a mixed hemlock and deciduous forest, passing over two small brooks and looping east of a small ridge. Crossing the first of two dirt roads (3.1 mi.), the trail ascends steeply to the top of a small ridge, before descending into a marshy, fairly open area drained by two small streams (3.3 mi.).

Shortly after, you will intersect with Risky Ranch Road (4.0 mi.). To connect with the **Broad Brook Trail**, follow the road approximately 0.3 mi. to the west (left) and look for a sign or blue blazes leading left from the road (downhill).

Just north of Risky Ranch Road, the AT/LT passes a side trail to the Seth Warner shelter (4.2 mi.). A short walk (0.2 mi.) west of the trail, the shelter has room for 6-8 people. A brook 350 feet west of the shelter provides water in spring, but is often dry during the summer months. A primitive camping area, with tent sites and a latrine, is located south on a spur trail from the shelter.

Hike 0.3 mi. north of the Seth Warner spur trail on the AT/LT to reach County Road (4.5 mi.), a dirt road between the towns of Pownal and Stamford, which is accessible from the east by car.

The AT/LT continues north 7.0 mi. to Congdon Camp and another 5.0 mi. to Route 9 in Vermont. For information on the Long Trail refer to the *Long Trail Guide* published by the Green Mountain Club.

BROAD BROOK TRAIL

Distances: 1.3 mi. to Agawon Trail, 3.7 mi. to Risky Ranch Rd.
Estimated time: 2.5 hours
Blazes: Blue
Map location: J – 22
Maintenance: Williams Outing Club

This watershed was once a source of drinking water for North Adams and Williamstown, but now has been incorporated into the Green Mountain National Forest. The trail follows the course of Broad Brook as it winds around and up the eastern side of the Dome, passing through rugged, heavily wooded country. There are several unbridged water crossings of the Brook and its tributaries, and travel may be difficult during spring or in wet weather.

HOW TO GET THERE

- Take Route 7 north towards Bennington.
- At 1.1 mi. you cross the Hoosic River flowing to the left (west).
- Turn right on Sand Springs Rd. at 1.6 miles. Keep right on main road until it becomes Bridges Road.
- Turn left on White Oaks Rd. (2.1 mi.) and drive uphill along Broad Brook.
- The pavement ends at the Vermont border (3.3 mi.). A pullout on the right marks the trailhead. The large pullout is also a school bus turn-around; be sure to leave space.

DESCRIPTION

The trail begins at the northern corner of the parking lot (0.0 mi.). It briefly joins a dirt road, before bearing right into the woods (0.1 mi.), where it parallels a spillway of the old North Adams waterworks. Stay on the right (east) side of the stream, winding through a hemlock and spruce forest before crossing the brook for the first time (1.1 mi.). At high water these crossings may be treacherous or impossible. Use caution.

Just before a second crossing (1.3 mi.), a signpost marks the junction with the **Agawon Trail**, which diverges to the left and ascends to join the **Dome Trail**. From here, you follow the brook. Bear right and carefully cross the current near two large boulders.

Many of the boulders in Broad Brook are quartzite, a very hard rock that resists weathering and erosion.

A double blaze marks a fork (1.5 mi.) where a high-water trail climbs away to the right. The main trail continues straight ahead and crosses the brook twice before merging with the high-water trail on the right side of the brook. At 1.8 mi. an old wagon track connected to Henderson Road joins from the right (southeast), and both cross the brook. The road then climbs away to the left (northwest), as the trail resumes its old course along the brook.

Continue on the northwest bank of Broad Brook, cross a small tributary (2.3 mi.), and climb steeply through a dense pine forest. Descend back to the valley floor, cross another small stream (2.4 mi.), and ascend the shoulder on the northwest side of the brook, passing through a hemlock grove.

When you arrive at the convergence of two streams forming Broad Brook (3.0 mi.), the trail follows the tributary to the east. Cross the north branch, climb a hill between the two streams, turn right (3.1 mi.), and then descend to and cross the tributary again (3.3 mi.). The trail terminates at Risky Ranch Road after 3.7 miles.

To the left (north), Risky Ranch Road intersects **County Road**, an unimproved road which connects Stamford and Pownal, VT. To the right (southeast) you will cross the **Long Trail/Appalachian Trail** in 0.3 miles. The **Seth Warner Shelter** is a quarter mile north of Risky Ranch Road.

For a long loop, you may hike south to the Pine Cobble Trailhead using the Appalachian Trail and **Pine Cobble Trail** (5.3 mi.). The Broad Brook trailhead is 3.0 mi. by road from the Pine Cobble trailhead.

DOME TRAIL

Distances: 1.2 miles to Agawon Trail, 2.6 miles to summit
Estimated time: 1.5 hours
Blazes: Red
Map location: J – 23
Maintenance: Williams Outing Club

Directly to the north of Williamstown, the Dome stands out among the surrounding mountains with its massive rounded summit. Although in Vermont, the Dome lures people from North Berkshire and forms a northern boundary of the area in this guide. The birch, maple, beech, and oaks of the lower slopes transition to a distinctly Laurentian plateau (referring to the "Laurentide" ice of the last glacial period) with boreal forest near the summit. Red spruce and balsam fir characterize this vegetation zone, common in northern Canada, but found only on the Dome and Mt. Greylock in the North Berkshire area. The visual contrast created by these vegetation changes is easily visible from the Williamstown valley floor.

HOW TO GET THERE
- From Field Park, drive north on Route 7 toward Pownal.
- At 1.1 mi. you cross the Hoosic River flowing to the left (west).
- Turn right on Sand Springs Rd. at 1.6 miles. Keep right on main road until it becomes Bridges Road.
- Turn left on White Oaks Rd. (2.1 mi.) and drive uphill along Broad Brook.
- The pavement ends at the Vermont border (3.3 mi.). Follow the dirt road farther uphill past a small reservoir to a pullout on the right (3.6 mi.). There is a sign and a road with a chain across.

DESCRIPTION
From White Oaks Road (0.0 mi.), follow an old wood road through a clearing and enter the forest heading east (0.2 mi.). The trail ascends steadily and at 0.5 mi. takes a sharp left (northwest) off the wood road (follow blazes). You pass through several Y intersections with logging roads and paths (follow blazes). Since erosion has stripped much of the soil in this section, watch your footing. Follow reroutes and try to avoid widening the trail.

At 1.2 mi. you reach a junction with the **Agawon Trail** (yellow blazes), which bears off to the right. Just beyond is Meeting House Rock (1.3 mi.), a large boulder that roughly marks the halfway point to the summit.

Continue past the boulder to an intersection marked by an abandoned truck (1.7 mi.). Bear right (northeast) and follow the marked trail over a series of small terraces and through several jogs left and right. Near the summit you emerge onto a ledge, dip down into a boggy area, and ascend to a last series of ledges that extend to the top of the mountain (2.6 mi.).

From the 2,748-foot summit you have a view somewhat screened by trees, but still magnificent, of the entire North Berkshire area. Unfold your map and pick out **Pine Cobble**, the **Greylock Range**, and the **Taconic Range**.

Between the spruce bog and the summit, blackberry and hobble-bush border the trail to welcome weary hikers in the fall. The flat top of the Dome is also attractive in winter when snow and frost cover every needle of the spruce and balsam fir.

AGAWON TRAIL

Distance: 0.7 miles, Dome Trail to Broad Brook Trail
Estimated time: 20–30 minutes
Blazes: Yellow
Map location: K - 24
Maintenance: Williams Outing Club

Williams College students cleared the Agawon Trail in the spring of 1959 to provide a route from Dome Trail to Broad Brook with a minimum of new trail mileage. Together the Dome, Agawon, and Broad Brook Trails form a pleasant 6.5 mi. circuit.

HOW TO GET THERE

- From the Dome Trail: Follow the Dome Trail for 1.2 mi. from its trailhead. The junction with the Agawon Trail, clearly marked with a trail sign, is on the right just below Meeting House Rock, an obvious large boulder.
- From the Broad Brook Trail: Before the second stream crossing from the White Oaks Road trailhead (1.3 mi.), a sign marks the Agawon trail junction to the left (northwest).

DESCRIPTION

From the **Dome Trail**, the Agawon Trail heads off to the northeast. After about 100 yards, follow a sharp right turn and descend. A small brook appears on the left before disappearing underground. The trail becomes steeper, eventually emerging onto a bluff overlooking Broad Brook. There it turns right and intersects with the **Broad Brook Trail** after a last 100 yards.

MOUNTAIN MEADOW PRESERVE

Distance: 4.5 miles of trails
Estimated time: Your choice
Blazes: Yellow and blue
Map location: H - 22
Maintenance: Trustees of Reservations, Williamstown Conservation Commission

Pamela B. Weatherbee donated some of the Williamstown portion of this preserve to the Trustees in 1998; the Pownal portion was purchased in 2000. The lands show signs of a widely variable history, including fields, gravel pits, and the ruins of two homes.

HOW TO GET THERE

Williamstown parking area:
- From Field Park, drive north on Route 7 toward Pownal.
- At 1.1 mi. you cross the Hoosic River flowing to the left (west).
- Turn right on Mason St. at 1.7 mi. and follow to entrance and parking (10 cars).

Pownal, VT, parking area:
- From Field Park, drive north on Route 7 toward Pownal.
- At 1.1 mi. you cross the Hoosic River flowing to the left (west).
- Turn right on Sand Springs Rd. at 1.6 miles. Keep right on main road until it becomes Bridges Road.
- Turn left on White Oaks Rd. (2.1 mi.) and drive uphill along Broad Brook.
- The pavement ends at the Vermont border (3.3 mi.). Follow the dirt road farther uphill and bear left at fork onto Benedict Rd. (3.5 mi.).
- Continue 0.1 mi. to entrance and parking (8 cars) on left.

DESCRIPTION

The 4.5 mile system of trails offers many options for short hikes. An information board, with maps of the property, is available at each of the parking lots. Many of the trails, particularly in the Pownal section, are suitable for cross-country skiing.

From the Williamstown parking area, access a loop around an open meadow with views of Greylock and the Taconics (0.8 mi), and a forested loop to an obstructed summit view (1.3 mi). This intriguing u-shaped hill was formed at the edge of melting glaciers about 14,500 years ago.

The Pownal lot provides access to loops from 0.3 mi to 2.0 mi. Check the map on the information board for points of interest, including obstructed views, gravel pits, and the ruins of two buildings. As you walk through the forest, look for old fence lines and stone walls, evidence that this land was once used for agriculture despite its gravelly soil.

TACONIC RANGE

The Taconic Mountain Range forms the western edge of North Berkshire, a north-to-south line shared with the Massachusetts-New York boundary. A series of regularly spaced stream valleys, locally referred to as "hollows," cut and drain each side of the range. During the 18th and 19th centuries, much of the forest was cleared to the Taconic Crest and nearly every hollow had a road climbing from Williamstown, up and over to New York. Today, forests have reclaimed farmland. Route 2 is the main east-west road over the range while many abandoned roads serve as the trails described in this section.

Like the Green Mountains, most of the Taconic Range is forested with northern hardwoods, but open meadows in some high areas offer excellent views of the surrounding mountains. From Berlin Mountain (2,798 feet), it is possible to see not only the Berkshires and the Green Mountains, but also the mountains along the Hudson – the Catskills, Helderbergs, and Adirondacks.

The principal trail in the Taconic Section is the Taconic Crest Trail, which runs 37 miles from Route 346 in North Petersburg, New York, to Route 20 in Hancock, Massachusetts. Three states and several non-profit groups have successfully purchased much of the ridge from private owners, but hikers should be aware that a few sections of the trail still cross private land. Please respect posted property in those areas.

Feeder trails from Williamstown to the Taconic Crest Trail include: the Birch Brook Trail, R.R.R. Brooks Trail, Shepherd's Well Trail, Sara Tenney Trail, Berlin Pass Trail, Class of '33 Trail, Phelps Trail, and Mills Hollow Trail. For full information concerning the entire Taconic Crest Trail, consult the *Taconic Crest Trail Guide*, or contact either the Taconic Hiking Club or the Williamstown Rural Lands Foundation.

HOPKINS FOREST LOOP TRAIL

Distances: 1.5 miles Lower Loop, 2.6 miles Upper Loop
Estimated time: 2 hours (both loops)
Map location: H – 20
Blazes: None
Maintenance: Williams College Center for Environmental Studies

Hopkins Memorial Forest is a 2,600-acre research site operated by the Williams College Center for Environmental Studies (CES). It includes a wide variety of forest types, from recently overgrown farmland to old woodlot stands of the 19th century. Old farm roads, stone walls, and partially visible cellar holes reflect the complex human history of the property.

Much of this information is recorded in *Farms to Forest*, a naturalist's guide published by the Center for Environmental Studies and available in local bookstores. This book also features a "guided" tour of the ecology of the lower loop trail. Research projects are in progress throughout the forest. To avoid disturbing them, please stay on trails and do not remove stakes, flags, or other markers.

The Hopkins Memorial Forest Loop Trail is actually a figure eight composed of a 1.5 mi. lower loop and 2.6 mi. upper loop.

HOW TO GET THERE

- From Field Park take Route 7 north to Bulkley Street (0.3 mi.).
- Turn left on Bulkley Street, cross a bridge over Hemlock Brook (0.4 mi.) and ascend a long gradual rise.
- When you reach the T-junction with Northwest Hill Road (1.1 mi.), turn right.
- The entrance to Hopkins Memorial Forest is on your left. Please park in the first parking area to the left.
- A few hundred feet beyond is the Rosenburg Center, which contains a small historical museum; and the Moon Barn, a historic structure that once stood on the farm in the center of Hopkins Memorial Forest belonging to Alfred C. Moon.

DESCRIPTION

The Lower Loop starts at the Moon Barn (0.0 mi.) along a carriage road improved by the Civilian Conservation Corps during the 1930s. Walk to the right past the Williams Outing Club Cabin (0.1 mi.), the HMF maple sugar operation, and an experimental weather station in a vestigial field. The trail winds through forest of various composition and age (refer to *Farms to Forest* for more natural history) before reaching a four-way intersection (0.8 mi.). A bench at this intersection is dedicated in memory of Williams College alumna Katie Craig '08, whose art appears in this book.

To return to the Moon Barn via the Lower Loop, turn left, away from the Upper Loop. This section of the trail may be a little swampy in the spring — please resist the temptation to trample the vegetation to either side. After a level section, the trail descends steeply back to the Rosenburg Center (1.5 mi.).

For a longer hike, venture on to the Upper Loop Trail (2.6 mi.). If in search of the **Birch Brook Trail**, follow the north (right) leg of the loop for a more direct approach. Otherwise, choose either path. The wide path was once a carriage road from which Amos Lawrence Hopkins would view his estate.

The trail crosses the middle and north branches of Birch Brook while passing through beautiful forest. This route allows a fantastic ski or snowshoe jaunt with enough snow, but take it in the clockwise direction. Upon returning to the four-way intersection, return along the Lower Loop for a 4.1 mi. total trip.

HOPKINS FOREST HOOSIC RIVER TRAIL

Distance: 1.5 miles
Estimated time: 1.5 hours (round trip)
Map location: G – 20
Blazes: None
Maintenance: Williams College Center for Environmental Studies

This trail follows the Hopkins Memorial Forests's eastern edge, along the Hoosic River, and passes abandoned structures of an old Williamstown Boys Club camp. It provides an easy hike or cross-country ski.

HOW TO GET THERE

- Follow directions to the Hopkins Forest Loop Trail.
- The trail begins a short distance beyond the parking area for the Hopkins Memorial Forest. Park there and continue by foot on Northwest Hill Road. After crossing the bridge over Ford Glen Brook, enter the woods on an old road to the right and pass under a cable gate.

DESCRIPTION

From the trail's entrance (0.0 mi.), walk east along the boundary of the Hopkins Memorial Forest, just north of Ford Glen Brook. At about 0.3 mi., enter a small, overgrown clearing around the remains of a boys club camp. Keep to the left of the basketball hoop — a trail between the hoop and pavilion leads to private property.

As you follow the trail, it settles along the Hoosic River and you may hear heavy equipment in the distance. The Williamstown wastewater treatment facility and Department of Public Works are located on the opposite bank. The trail gradually curves left, following a grade well above the river.

After passing through rich bottom-land forest and crossing a stream (0.8 mi.), the trail drops down to the bank of the river and into a dense stand of hemlock (1.0 mi.). Once past the hemlocks, the forest allows in more sun and is overgrown with shrubs; evidence of clearing in the not-too-distant past. Continue along the riverbank and out into actively farmed fields (1.5 mi.) The far side of these fields is private property; please return the way you came.

BIRCH BROOK TRAIL

Distance: 1.4 miles
Estimated time: 1 hour
Map location: E – 21
Blazes: Blue
Maintenance: Williams Outing Club, Williams College Center for Environmental Studies

This spur trail to the Taconic Crest Trail takes you through the Hopkins Memorial Forest from the Loop Trail. The trail begins at the north branch of Birch Brook, its namesake.

HOW TO GET THERE
- Follow directions to the Hopkins Forest Loop Trail.
- Hike the lower loop to the four-way intersection (1.0 mi.), turn right, and proceed to the Birch Brook Trail (1.7 mi.).

DESCRIPTION
From the trail entrance (0.0 mi.), the trail heads west, briefly paralleling the North Branch of Birch Brook before jogging north, away from the stream. You hike mostly on old road grades with intermittent reroutes to avoid heavily eroded sections.

There are several beautiful patches of ferns along the trail as you climb toward the Taconic Crest. The forest in this area is susceptible to blowdowns during storms. If trees block the trail, try to go over, rather than around, and please report trail conditions to the Williams Outing Club.

Shortly after crossing the Massachusetts-New York border, the Birch Brook Trail terminates at a signpost marking the junction with the **Taconic Crest Trail** at 1.5 miles.

The Snow Hole is 1.6 mi. north and North Petersburg, NY, is 4.5 mi. farther. To the south are the **Shepherd's Well Trail** (0.6 mi.) and Route 2 (1.1 mi.).

BUXTON RAVINE TRAIL (HATTON TRAIL)
Distance: 1 mile
Estimated time: 1 hour
Map location: G – 19
Blazes: Light blue
Maintenance: Williamstowntown Conservation Commission

This short trail provides in-town access to the Hunter Family Loop of the Sara Tenney Trail, and in turn, many of the Taconic Range's local trails.

HOW TO GET THERE
- From Field Park, head west on Main St. (0.7).
- Continue on to Petersburg Rd.
- Park in a small gravel pull-off on the left (0.75 mi.)
- The trailhead begins here at the stream's edge.

DESCRIPTION

At the gravel parking area, note a yellow sign near the stream: "Town of Williamstown Conservation Land." The trail begins here at the stream's edge. Cross over the stream and into a Hemlock stand. Begin walking uphill (south) through a beech and maple forest, eventually working your way to a small ridge line on the left. The trail joins an old woods road (0.2 mi.), and soon after, another old woods road merges into the trail as well. Head right (west) at 0.4 mi., and cross a small seasonal stream. The trail levels out at 0.5 mi. but again ascends another old woods road and into the Taconic Trail State Park at 1.0 mi., which is also the junction with the **Hunter Family Loop Trail**.

SHEEP HILL

Distance: 0.1 to 1.5 miles
Estimated time: Up to 2 hours
Map location: G – 17
Blazes: None
Maintenance: Williamstown Rural Lands Foundation

Sheep Hill, a former dairy farm, is the headquarters of the Williamstown Rural Lands Foundation and offers hiking, snowshoeing, educational materials and events, and skiing on an old Williams College ski hill.

HOW TO GET THERE
- From Field Park, take Route 7 south.
- Turn right at Sheep Hill, immediately after crossing the third bridge (1.0 mi.).
- Parking is available at the bottom of the drive, and beyond the farmhouse behind the garage.

DESCRIPTION

Information can be found at the map board outside the farmhouse. Check inside the house and barns for more educational materials and exhibits.

The **Meadow Walk** follows the lower portion of the hill for a short, easy loop.

The **Rosenburg Ramble** is a 1.5 mi. loop around the perimeter of the fields, including two parking areas along the hill's top edge. These are also accessible from Bee Hill Road and offer panoramic views of the Greylock range. Bee Hill Road also provides access to the **Fitch Trail** and **Running Pine Trail** for extended hikes.

FITCH TRAIL

Distances: 0.7 mile to Bee Hill Road, 1.1 miles to R.R.R. Brooks Trail
Estimated time: 30 minutes to Bee Hill
Blazes: Blue
Map location: G – 18
Maintenance: Williamstown Rural Lands Foundation

For a short hike you can ascend Bee Hill through the Edward H. Fitch Memorial Woodlands protected by the Williamstown Rural Lands Foundation and the Massachusetts Department of Conservation and Recreation. For a pleasant loop, link up with the R.R.R. Brooks Trail and return to your car along Bee Hill Road.

HOW TO GET THERE
- From the intersection of Routes 2 and 7, take Route 7 south.
- Turn right on Bee Hill Road (0.6 mi.).
- At 1.3 mi. a wooden sign on the right marks a small lot for hiker parking. If this lot is full, continue along the road for another 0.3 mi. and you will find two additional pulloffs to the left.

DESCRIPTION
From the north side of the parking lot (0.0 mi.), follow the well-marked path on gentle grades through young forest. Watch for educational signs and their corresponding plots to learn about the forest.

Just before crossing a stone wall, pass the **Running Pine Trail** (0.3 mi), an alternate route back to Bee Hill Rd. At 0.7 mi., crest the rounded top of Bee Hill, where only a few decades ago you would have had a clear view of the **Greylock Range** and valley below.

For a 2.4 mi. loop, continue over the west side of the hill to meet up with the **R.R.R. Brooks Trail** (1.1 mi.). Turn right to reach Bee Hill Rd. (1.9 mi.) through Flora Glen. To return to your car, turn right and walk 0.5 mi. uphill to the Fitch Trail parking lot.

RUNNING PINE TRAIL

Distance: 0.65 miles
Estimated time: 30 minutes
Blazes: Blue
Map location: G – 18
Maintenance: Williamstown Rural Lands Foundation

Originally designed for cross-country skiers, this short spur trail winds away from, and returns to, the Fitch Trail.

HOW TO GET THERE
• Refer to directions for the Fitch Trail (page 78).

DESCRIPTION
From the Fitch Trail parking area (0.0 mi.), follow the Fitch Trail. At 0.1 mi., turn left at the junction where Running Pine Trail branches. Follow a set of small stone steps uphill and zig-zag your way through as many as ten switchbacks in quick succession. At 0.6 mi., note a large stone wall running adjacent the trail, and also Massachusetts State Forest boundary markers, which are blue (similar to the Running Pine Trail's blazes). Walk alongside the wall, keeping it to your left, until you reach the trail's end at another junction with the Fitch Trail. Turn left to continue on to the Bee Hill summit and the **R.R.R. Brooks Trail**, or turn right to return to the parking area on Bee Hill Road.

R.R.R. BROOKS TRAIL

Distances: 1.8 miles to Old Petersburg Road, 2.4 miles to Shepherd's Well Trail, 2.9 miles to Route 2
Estimated time: 2.0 hours
Map location: G – 18
Blazes: Blue
Maintenance: Williams Outing Club

Running parallel to Route 2, this trail offers hikers a direct route from Williamstown to Petersburg Pass, passing through the 930-acre Taconic Trail State Park along the way. R.R.R. Brooks is named for a former dean of Williams College who lived on Bee Hill Road and originally cleared the trail. One of the highlights is Flora Glen, a beautiful wooded area that is believed to have been the inspiration for William Cullen Bryant's poem *Thanatopsis*.

HOW TO GET THERE

- From the intersection of Routes 2 and 7, take Route 7 south.
- Turn right on Bee Hill Road (0.6 mi.) and drive up the hill and over a bridge. A sign marks the trailhead.
- Parking is available on the road just north of the bridge, or continue along Bee Hill Road to the Fitch Trail lot (1.3 mi.) or one of the pullouts beyond it on the left.

DESCRIPTION

Although the **Fitch Trail** provides access to the R.R.R. Brooks Trail and makes a nice 1.8 mi. loop, this description will assume you have walked 0.5 mi. down Bee Hill Rd. to the trailhead, or been dropped off.

The trail begins at the south end of a defunct dam (0.0 mi.) and skirts a former pond, drained in 1997. This section borders private property, so please be respectful and walk only on the trail. Here is Flora Glen, nearly always wet, and a sea of ferns during the spring and summer months.

Vegetation alternates between northern hardwood (mostly maple, beech, and birch) and evergreen (spruce and hemlock) as you walk along the south side above the stream. The trail descends to the level of the stream (0.5 mi.), and makes an abrupt left (0.6 mi.) to climb steeply up a series of steps out of the streambed. At 0.8 mi., the Fitch Trail enters from the left.

After a bridge (0.9 mi.), you pass through a forest of birch and beech trees, and emerge at the edge of a large field (1.4 mi.). A sign identifies the R.R.R Brooks Trail for descending hikers.

Hike uphill (west) through the field and stay left (south) of the tree island. Tall grass can make for difficult navigation across this open area. Your path and Route 2 will gradually converge towards the Old Petersburg Rd. and the **Sara Tenney Trail** (1.8 mi.). If you are misplaced when you hit this double track jeep road, walk toward Route 2 (south) to pick up the upper section of R.R.R Brooks.

Across Route 2 from Old Petersburg Road is a pull-out where a vehicle shuttle could be arranged. To continue toward the Taconic Crest, enter the woods 50 feet from Route 2 on a wide path marked by a sign and blue blazes. It runs parallel to Route 2 up a gentle ascent.

At 2.4 mi. you will reach the junction with the **Shepherd's Well Trail**. To the left, the R.R.R Brooks Trail continues on a dirt road until it makes a short descent to the left and dead-ends near a steep drop by Route 2 (2.9 mi.). There is no parking at Route 2. The Petersburg Pass Scenic area is 0.4 mi. west along the road.

SARA TENNEY TRAIL AND SKI LOOPS
Distances: 4.0 miles
Estimated time: 3 hours
Blazes: Blue
Map location: G – 18
Maintenance: Williamstown Conservation Commission

Designed for cross-country skiers, this system of trails follows old roads and alternate paths from Flora Glen up to the parking lot at Petersburg Pass Scenic Area.

HOW TO GET THERE
• Refer to the directions for the RRR Brooks Trail.

DESCRIPTION
Begin at the **R.R.R. Brooks** trailhead and cross the braided stream at 0.1 mi. Before crossing back over to the south side of the brook (0.2 mi), follow blue blazes up a steep bank to the right. Here, the trail skirts the edge of private property. Please stay on the trail.

The first section of trail climbs the steep banks of Flora Glen, and skiers may need to hike or use climbing-skins. After climbing through a stand of hemlock, the trail meets an old road (0.4 mi). Directly ahead is the **Smith Trail**, a short spur cut in 2018. (Note: this trail not marked on the map as of 2019 printing.)

The Smith Trail follows blue blazes for 0.3 mi. on Williamstown

Conservation Land. There are two nice views. One, about halfway along the trail at the forest's edge (adjacent a private landowner's property), affords views of the Greylock masif. The second view is at the trail's terminus near a small rocky outcropping and provides a distinct view of the Williams College campus from the west.

To continue on the Sara Tenney Trail, turn left on the old road and on to an intersection (0.5 mi.). To the right (north) is the **Hunter Family Loop** and **Bob's Ski Loop**, and to the left (south) is the Sara Tenney Trail, an easier route that follows an old woods road.

The Hunter Family Loop, furthest to the north, climbs gradually up Birch Hill. Take care as you cross a property boundary (1.0 mi.) because it is marked with blue paint similar to the trail blazes. Follow a switchback and meet Bob's Ski Loop at 1.2 mi.

Bob's Ski Loop follows the eastern ridge up Birch Hill. Pass an intersection with the Hunter Family Loop and a bypass to the southern route of the Sara Tenney Trail (0.9 mi.). Continue up the ridge, across the top of Birch Hill, and meet an old road (1.2 mi.). Follow the road out to a field maintained by the Deparment of Conservation and Recreation, and an intersection with the Sara Tenney Trail (1.6 mi.).

From the intersection (noted earlier) at 0.5 mi., the Sara Tenney Trail follows an old road along the south side of Birch Hill. At 1.1 mi., it intersects another forest road, which begins a graded bypass up to Bob's Ski Loop to the north. Continue on the Sara Tenney Trail into an open field (1.3 mi.), pass Bob's Ski Loop to the right (1.4 mi.), and continue through the fields to the Old Petersburg Road and a gate at Route 2 (1.9 mi.).

Cross over Route 2 to the parking area on its far side. Just past the end of the guard rail on the downhill (east) side, the trail resumes into the woods (2.0 mi). Follow the path down into Treadwell Hollow. An alternate route, for easier skiing, heads to the left at 2.1 mi. and re-connects at 2.3 mi.

The trail heads down a bank and meets an old woods road (2.4 mi.) and immediately crosses **Hemlock Brook**. Follow the road as it parallels the brook until it crosses two branches in quick succession over partially exposed culverts (2.9 mi.). Here, the trail has been rerouted: turn southwest on an historic woods road (Leete Farm) indicated by a sign for the Sara Tenney Trail to Petersburg

Pass. If you instead continue north of Hemlock Brook, the trail has been abandoned due to the complete failure of the road's drainage infrastructure.

At 3.2 mi., pass above an abandoned house, sold to the state by Sara Tenney in the 1950s after the town gave up maintaining the road's many stream crossings. Continue on the road, past a post marking the NY/MA border (3.8 mi.). This road, buried by the expansion of Route 2, dead-ends in the woods below the parking lot at Petersburg Pass Scenic Area (4.0 mi.).

To walk the trail in reverse, you can find its trailhead at the southeast corner of the Petersburg Pass Scenic Area parking lot.

TENNEY HILL TRAIL
Distances: 1.3 miles
Estimated time: 45 minutes
Map location: E – 18
    (Note: trail not marked on map as of 2019 printing)
Blazes: Blue
Maintenance: Williamstown Rural Lands Foundation

The 178-acre Tenney Woodland Preserve was donated by the Tenney family to the Williamstown Rural Lands Foundation in 2017, and this trail was cut soon after in 2018. The path takes hikers up to the top of a small peak before depositing them down onto the old Bee Hill Road extension between Route 2 and Berlin Road.

HOW TO GET THERE
- Take Routes 7 and 2 southwest to where they split (2.3 mi.).
- Follow Route 2 west to the first pulloff on the left (south) side of Route 2 (4.5 mi.).

DESCRIPTION
Just past the guard rail on the downhill (east) side of the parking pulloff, there is a trailhead for both the Tenney Hill Trail and the **Sara Tenney Trail** to Petersburg Pass via Treadwell Hollow. The trail on the left (east side) is the Tenney Hill Trail (0.0 mi.).

Begin hiking on a slightly elevated ridge beneath a high canopy of red oaks. After a quick descent into denser, mixed forest, the trail commits to a consistent uphill for the next quarter-mile. Follow the trail through a couple of switchbacks before heading south to the hike's high point at a grassy knoll (0.3 mi.). This open area features young birch and striped maple trees beneath more mature oaks and sugar maples. Hay-scented fern is scattered throughout this clearing.

Continue up and over, passing to the right of a huge old oak tree (0.4 mi.) as you begin your descent. Hike east through open forest before entering a denser beech forest and following a switch-back west-southwest. Notice the steep fallaway pitch to your left as you walk along a ridge that allows views into, and down onto, the forest's canopy (0.8 mi.). Not long after, on your right (west), a rock ledge drop precipitously to the forest floor. Observe how trees grow overtop the moss-covered rock.

Hike past to the south-soutwest, following a quick switchback before descending down off the ridge into the forest below. At 1.0 mi., take a short, steep downhill before heading generally south as you wind your way steadily downhill before encountering the old Bee Hill Road extension (1.3 mi.). Head back the way you came, or turn right to eventually reach Berlin Road, where you can link up with the **Turnpike** and **Sara Tenney Trails** to return to your car.

SHEPHERD'S WELL TRAIL

Distance: 1.0 mile to Taconic Crest Trail
Estimated time: 40 minutes
Map location: D – 19
Blazes: Blue
Maintenance: Williams Outing Club

HOW TO GET THERE
• Via the R.R.R. Brooks Trail or the Taconic Crest Trail.

DESCRIPTION
From the **R.R.R. Brooks Trail** junction (0.0 mi.), the Shepherd's Well Trail branches to the right and climbs gently through a forest of maple, beech and oak trees.

A white sign indicates the boundary of **Hopkins Memorial Forest** (0.4 mi.). As you enter the forest, notice the red and yellow bands painted on the trees. These are part of a permanent grid system for vegetation surveys, established by the United States Forest Service in 1936 and still maintained by Williams College professors and students.

Just beyond a double blaze signaling an abrupt left turn, the trail enters an open area filled with huckleberries and blueberries. The spectacular view encompasses the **Greylock Range** to the east and the **Taconic Range**, the **Old Williams Ski Area** and **Petersburg Pass** to the south.

Across the clearing, the trail levels off, descends gradually and turns right (0.9 mi.) to skirt the ridge. To the right was once a well belonging to a farmer named Shepherd, but all traces of it have now disappeared.

Follow the contour around the rise in the ridge to meet the **Taconic Crest Trail** at a trail sign (1.0 mi.).

MARGARET LINDLEY PARK TRAILS
Distance: 0.9 mile
Estimated time: 40 minutes
Blazes: Blue, yellow, pink, and red.
Map location: F – 16
Maintenance: Williamstown Conservation Commission

This trail network rolls gently through shaded hemlock forest and along the banks of Hemlock Brook.

HOW TO GET THERE
- From the intersection of Rts. 2 and 7 in Williamstown (the roundabout):
- Take Routes 7 and 2 southwest (2.3 mi.).
- Turn right (west) into Margaret Lindley Park just after Route 2 leaves Route 7 (2.31 mi.).

DESCRIPTION
From the parking area, walk to the far side of the swimming pond, to the trailhead at the forest's edge (0.0 mi.). The trail system consists of a main loop, the Torrey Woods Trail, with spurs leading to other points of interest. Follow blue blazes for the Torrey Woods

Trail. At 0.1 mi., reach a four-way junction. Turn right and cross a large wooden bridge. Continue straight past a right turn uphill (0.2 mi.) with pink blazes marking the way to an alternate parking area on Torrey Woods Road, and continue along the brook. Make a slight right turn up and away from the brook and cross a footbridge (ignoring another right turn, again to the Torrey Woods Road parking area). Cross a third footbridge and, soon after, a fourth, before fording Hemlock Brook on large step-stones (0.6 mi.). At the far bank, turn left to continue. Walk through riparian habitat and eventually pass a spur trail on your right (0.8 mi.), blazed yellow. This trail leads to Sweet Brook Road and Harmon Pond. Continue straight to stay on the Torrey Woods Trail and return to the Park (0.9 mi.).

To hike to Sweet Brook Road and Harmon Pond, take the yellow-blazed spur trail and walk for less than 0.1 mi. up and away from the stream onto a plateau. Pass a small vernal pool and arrive at Sweet Brook Road. Cross over the road to reach the **Harmon Pond Trail** (orange blazes) or continue on the yellow-blazed trail to loop back down to the four-way junction on the Torrey Woods Trail. As you approach the junction, there is a spur trail blazed red. This path takes you directly to the parking lot at Margaret Lindley Park through an especially impressive stand of hemlock trees.

HARMON POND TRAIL
Distances: 0.3 miles
Estimated time: 20 minutes
Map location: F – 16
   (Note: trail not marked on map as of 2019 printing)
Blazes: Orange
Maintenance: Williamstown Rural Lands Foundation

Harmon Pond and its deep hemlock forest is a gem of the north Berkshire County hiking area. This trail can be hiked on its own or combined with the paths winding through the Margaret Lindley Park for a longer hike.

HOW TO GET THERE

- From the intersection of Routes 7 and 2 in Williamstown, follow Route 7 south.
- Turn right on Woodcock Road (2.8 mi.).
- Turn right on Sweet Brook Road (3.3 mi.) and follow to its terminus. Park on the edge of the street (3.7 mi.).

DESCRIPTION

After parking, walk to the south side of the road where a small sign marks the start of the Harmon Pond Trail (0.0 mi.). As you walk through the shade of the hemlock forest, notice the vernal pools to your left, and turn to cross over via a small bog bridge. Not long after, the trail winds back to the right (west) and you dip through another damp crossing before turning left to head away from the moist part of the forest.

Reach a sign-posted intersection (0.1 mi.) and turn left (south) towards the pond. As you approach the water's edge, tuck through a tunnel of young hemlock trees towered over by mature white pines (0.2 mi.). Soon you arrive at the pond as the trail follows its banks eastward and across a log footbrige. As you walk, look carefully for red spruce saplings, a species found more commonly at higher elevations. Cross through a small ravine before heading uphill as the pond's bank falls away to the water below. Exit the forest (0.3 mi.) via a short, steep descent towards the dam, where the trail ends. To return, you can retrace your steps. Or, for a longer walk of about one extra mile, you can continue across the grass to a metal gate and Harmon Pond Road. (Note: Harmon Pond Road is a private road and no parking is allowed.) Follow the road to its terminus at Woodcock Road and take a right turn. Soon after, Sweet Brook Road is on your right, which you can follow back to your car.

TURNPIKE TRAIL

Distance: 0.9 mile
Estimated time: 40 minutes
Blazes: None until 0.75 mi.; then, blue
Map location: D – 18
Maintenance: Williamstown Conservation Commission

This trail, which takes advantage of one of the better preserved woods roads in town, provides access to the Sara Tenney Trail and Treadwell Hollow.

HOW TO GET THERE

- From the intersection of Rts. 2 and 7 in Williamstown, take Route 7 south (2.2 mi.).
- Turn right on Route 2 west.
- Turn left on Torrey Woods Road (2.5 mi.).
- Continue on Berlin Road (2.9 mi.), where the surface changes from pavement to dirt.
- Look carefully on the right for a small gravel pull-off and a large metal gate (4.3 mi.). Park here.

DESCRIPTION

The trail starts at a large metal gate (0.0 mi.). Walk past it onto an old woods road and continue through a young beech forest. At 0.1 mi., another woods road joins from the left. Continue straight. Soon after, note an old stone wall on either side of the trail (0.3 mi.), with a very large oak growing through the wall on the right side of the trail. The trail begins a gentle curve left (0.4 mi.) into more mature forest. Cross into Massachusetts State Forest at 0.8 mi., a boundary marked by blue diamond blaze markers. At this point in the trail, light blue paint blazes mark the way. Cross a small stream near a fern-filled glade and, soon after, reach the junction with the **Sara Tenney Trail** (0.9 mi.). Turn left to access the **Taconic Crest Trail**. Turn right to access a parking area on Route 2.

WRLF LOOP TRAIL
Distance: 1.4 miles
Estimated time: 1 hour
Blazes: Blue diamond markers
Map location: C – 17
Maintenance: Williamstown Rural Lands Foundation

During the summer of 1998, the Williamstown Rural Lands Foundation designed and installed this short interpretive loop trail. Small signs along the trail offer natural history information to hikers.

HOW TO GET THERE
- Refer to directions for the Class of '33 Trail (page 90).

DESCRIPTION
From the parking area you may start directly on the Haley Brook Cut-off Trail for a shorter loop, including a spur trail to a deck overlooking a waterfall, or walk 400 feet back down the road you drove in on to the Loop Trail and **Class of '33 Trail** trailhead.

Each trail is well blazed to and across **Haley Brook** to a relatively level logging grade south of the brook. On the road, walk west. To the left (south) you will pass four old pits used to make charcoal from trees on this land. The trail ends at the **Old Williams College Ski Area** and you may retrace your steps or return via Berlin Road.

CLASS OF '33 OR BERLIN MOUNTAIN TRAIL
Distances: 2.0 miles
Estimated time: 1.5 hours
Blazes: Blue
Map location: C – 17
Maintenance: Williams Outing Club

Members of the Williams Outing Club constructed this trail up Berlin Mountain in the fall of 1933. Slightly longer than the route via the Berlin Pass Trail, it is an extremely pretty – though arduous – hike through classic New England mountain woods.

HOW TO GET THERE

- Take Routes 7 and 2 southwest to where they split (2.3 mi.).
- Turn right (west) on Route 2 and then left on Torrey Woods Road (2.6 mi.).
- At the first intersection, continue straight (3.0 mi.).
- At a fork (3.8 mi.) follow the left road (Berlin Mountain Road) uphill and past a number of houses to the trailhead, clearly signed on the left.
- There is room to park 2-3 cars about 400 feet beyond on the left (4.7 mi.).

DESCRIPTION

From the parking area is a cut-off for the **Williamstown Rural Lands Foundation** (WRLF) **Loop Trail**. To access the Class of '33 trail or the entire Loop Trail, walk 400 feet back the way you drove in. On the south side is a signed trailhead (0.0 mi.) and a trail blazed with blue paint swatches (WOC) as well as blue diamond markers (WRLF).

Follow blazes through left and right turns to Haley Brook and the first interpretive sign of the WRLF Loop Trail (0.2 mi.). Cross the brook and climb the far bank to a well-signed junction. Bear left (east) to stay on the Class of '33 Trail, where the Loop Trail continues to the right. Follow blazes uphill and right (south) through hemlocks and up a deeply gullied logging grade (0.4 mi.) to a level area and hemlock grove.

Descend to the site of the old Williams Outing Club Berlin Cabin marked by remains of an outhouse (0.7 mi.). Heed a sharp right switchback to the brook, and after crossing and hiking briefly uphill on a footpath, meet a logging grade on the far side. Turn right and then bear left to follow a steady steep grade to the mountain ridge above. At 1.2 mi. you will gain the ridge leading west to the summit of Berlin Mountain.

Logging in the years 1995-1997 widened old woods roads in a confusing network. Large blue blazes mark a boundary line, not the trail that follows the ridgeline logging road. If you start to head downhill, you are going the wrong way. Stay high on the ridge. At 1.5 mi. is a fantastic view of **Broad Brook** and the **Dome** to the northeast.

At 1.8 mi. continue straight on the ridge towards the summit.

One last turn left up the top of the **Old Williams College Ski Area** will bring you to the clear summit of Berlin Mountain (2.0 mi.).

Four small cement piers mark the site of an old fire tower. A panoramic view northeast-to-southeast includes all the areas described in this guide. To the southwest are the rolling hills of Southeast Hollow, with the Catskills rising in the distance. Albany and Troy are visible to the west and on a clear day you might see the southern Adirondacks to the northwest.

There are three options for return to the parking lot. You may retrace your route on the Class of '33 Trail for a 4.0 mi. roundtrip. Alternatively, instead of taking your first right onto the '33 Trail, continue straight (north-northeast) down the abandoned ski slope (3.5 mi. total). This route is unmaintained and extremely steep. Use caution.

Finally, you may follow the **Taconic Crest Trail** (white and blue diamond markers) north to the **Berlin Pass Trail** and back to your vehicle (4.3 mi.).

BULLOCK TRAIL
Distances: 1.0 mile
Estimated time: 45 minutes
Map location: C – 17
    (Note: trail not marked on map as of 2019 printing)
Blazes: Yellow
Maintenance: Williamstown Conservation Commission

This trail runs parallel, and at a slightly higher elevation than, much of the Williamstown Rural Lands Foundation Loop Trail. The trail makes use of old logging roads as it passes through airy stands of sugar maple and birch trees on its way to the Old Williams College Ski Area.

HOW TO GET THERE
• Refer to directions for the Class of '33 Trail (page 90).

DESCRIPTION
From the parking area is a cut-off for the **Williamstown Rural**

Lands Foundation (WRLF) **Loop Trail**. To access the Bullock Trail, the **Class of '33** trail, or the entire Loop Trail, walk 400 feet back the way you drove in. On the south side is a signed trailhead (0.0 mi.) and a trail blazed with blue paint swatches (WOC) as well as blue diamond markers (WRLF).

Follow blazes through left and right turns to Haley Brook (0.2 mi.). Cross the brook and climb the far bank to a well-signed junction. Bear left (east) to stay on the Class of '33 Trail. Soon after, the Bullock trailhead is on your right (0.3 mi.), marked by yellow blazes. Follow the old forest road as it makes its way gradually uphill. As you hike, note how swaths of sweet-smelling hay-scented fern populate beneath openings in the canopy overhead. Two small seeps cross the trail near 0.5 mi., and farther along, a small stand of hemlock trees provides a shady resting spot (0.7 mi.). At 0.8 mi., the trail merges with another old road. Keep a sharp eye for the trail as it makes a slight left turn up towards a steeper grade (marked by a double blaze). At 1.0 mi., the hill finally levels, just within sight of the **Old Williams College Ski Area**. You can retrace your steps from here, or continue hiking down the ski hill to connect with the WRLF Loop Trail or Berlin Road.

BERLIN PASS TRAIL

Distances: 0.8 mi. to Berlin Pass, 2.0 mi. to Berlin Mountain
Estimated time: 45 minutes to Berlin Pass
Blazes: Blue
Map location: C – 18
Maintenance: Williams Outing Club

For an afternoon hike or direct access to the Taconic Crest Trail, try the Berlin Pass Trail. It was once a section of the Boston-Albany post road, one of two dozen such roads through the Berkshires that were used to deliver everything from newspapers to packages. A one mile walk leads to wind-swept meadows with panoramic views almost equivalent to those of the Class of '33 Trail.

HOW TO GET THERE
- Take Routes 7 and 2 southwest to where they split (2.3 mi.).
- Turn right (west) on Route 2 and then left on Torrey Woods

Road (2.6 mi.).
* At the first intersection, continue straight (3.0 mi.).
* At a fork (3.8 mi.), follow the left road (Berlin Mountain Road).
* Continue straight to a dead end below the Old Williams College Ski Area (5.1 mi.).
* Park on the right side of the ski area parking lot.

DESCRIPTION

From the ski area parking lot (0.0 mi.), follow a jeep road into the woods on the north (right, when driving into the parking lot) side. The trail swings west through a mixed hardwood forest of ash, sugar maple, poplar, and red oak. Just off to the right at 0.2 mi. is a gray stone pillar marking the boundary between Massachusetts and New York.

As the trail continues to climb, soil grows rockier and the composition of the forest begins to change; beech and paper birch mix with oak, hop hornbeam and red maple. After crossing a brook, the trail emerges into the brushy saddle known as Berlin Pass.

At Berlin Pass, the old stage route crosses the **Taconic Crest Trail** (TCT) before descending the western slope of the Taconic Range to Berlin, New York. If you continue on the TCT, which runs north-south across the pass, **Berlin Mountain** is 1.2 mi. south and **Petersburg Pass** is 1.5 mi. to the north.

For a loop back to the parking lot, you may climb Berlin Mountain and then descend via the steep and unmaintained **Old Williams College Ski Area** (3.0 mi.) or the **Class of '33 Trail** (4.5 mi.).

OLD WILLIAMS COLLEGE SKI AREA

Distance: 1.0 mile
Estimated time: 45 minutes
Blazes: None
Map location: B – 18
Maintenance: None

Williams College cut this extremely steep ski trail in the old New England tradition: steep, narrow, and winding. NCAA Division

I skiers from across New England raced this course in the 1960s and 1970s. Today, most hikers use this trail as a descent route to complete a loop with the Class of '33 Trail or Berlin Pass Trail, and in the winter it is used by backcountry skiers.

HOW TO GET THERE

- Take Routes 7 and 2 south to where they diverge (2.3 mi.).
- Turn right (west) on Route 2 and then left on Torrey Woods Road (2.6 mi.).
- At the first intersection, continue straight (3.0 mi.).
- At a fork (3.8 mi.) follow the left-hand road (Berlin Mountain Road) uphill and past a number of houses.
- Continue straight to a dead end below the Old Williams College Ski Area (5.1 mi.).

DESCRIPTION

Most people use this route for a descent; but if you want a punishing uphill grunt, this is the trail for you. To find the trail coming down from Berlin Mountain, refer to the **Class of '33 Trail** description.

An obvious clear area heads directly up the steep north side of Berlin Mountain, south of the parking area (0.0 mi.). Dirt bikes have created a number of trails up the slope — choose your course.

Above, the ski slope narrows and winds through a series of turns. Look down and imagine racing around these bends on skis! Near the summit of Berlin Mountain, the Class of '33 Trail merges from the left (0.9 mi.). A short walk farther takes you to the summit, a fantastic view at the site of an old fire tower and the **Taconic Crest Trail**.

MOUNT GREYLOCK REGIONAL SCHOOL TRAILS

Distance: 1.3 miles of trails
Estimated time: 1 hour
Blazes: None
Map location: F – 15
Maintenance: Mount Greylock Regional School, Williams College, Sweetwood of Williamstown

This small network of wide trails is used for training and racing by the Mount Greylock Regional School cross-country running and skiing teams, as well as the Williams College cross-country running team.

HOW TO GET THERE

- From the intersection of Rts. 2 and 7 in Williamstown, take Route 7 south to Mount Greylock Regional School (3.4 mi.).
- Turn right at the school and park.
- Walk behind the school to the football field.
- The trails begin near the south side of the field: there is a mowed, uphill trail through the grass heading southwest (less than 0.1 mi.) past the football field. It leads to a wooden bench. This is the trailhead.

DESCRIPTION

From the trail's start at the wooden bench (0.0 mi.), hike into the woods on a wide trail lined with wood chips. After 0.3 mi., the trail makes an abrupt 90-degree turn (east) downhill and winds back to the football field (0.5 mi.). Hug the tree line on your left and continue walking past the field before re-entering the woods (0.6 mi.). Pass briefly through a grassy field before committing again to the woods trail under a maple canopy, heading northeast. Hike down a short, steep hill before curving right and notice an old stone wall extending on either side of the trail. Continue, keeping the wall on your right as you now head uphill, cresting at a T-junction (0.8 mi.).

Left will take you downhill along a utility line before looping back south (0.9 mi.) near the Sweetwood Retirement Community. Hug the tree line on your right for 60 yards and re-enter the woods on an uphill trail. Reach the hill's crest (1.1 mi.). Just past it is another junction: head straight to exit the woods down to the high school's playing fields, near where you started; or turn right (north) and continue on the woods trail down Hil's Hill. Another T-junction awaits (1.3 mi.). A right turn will take you 125 yards to the previous T-junction (just prior the utility line and Sweetwood Retirement Community). Left will continue the trail and bring you to its exit near the northeast side of the football fields.

FIELD FARM

Distance: 4.5 miles of trails
Estimated time: Your choice
Blazes: Yellow
Map location: D – 13
Maintenance: The Trustees of Reservations

The Trustees of Reservations manage this 316 acre property that has been farmed continuously since the founding of Williamstown. It is home to two modernist houses: the Guest House, which is run as a bed and breakfast; and The Folly, which is open for tours in the summer. A 4.5 mi. system of loop trails visits the varied habitats on this terrace formed in glacial Lake Bascom about 14,500 years ago. A suggested donation of $2.00 helps to maintain the trails.

HOW TO GET THERE

- Take Route 7 south from Williamstown to Five Corners (4.1 mi.), the junction with Route 43 (flashing light).
- Turn right on Route 43, and immediately right on Sloan Road (west).
- One mile up Sloan Road is the signed entrance to Field Farm (5.1 mi. on the right).
- Enter the property and take the first right to an information board and parking area.

DESCRIPTION

At the trailhead are a small nature center and an information board with maps to the 4.5 mi. network of trails. All trails are marked with yellow blazes and green-and-white directional signs. Take a short walk on the **Pond Trail** for views of wetland wildlife. The **South Trail** offers a 1.5 mi. round trip, beginning with a walk along the edge of a wetland and excellent views of the Greylock range to the east.

The **North Trail**, **Oak Loop**, and **Caves Trail** offer loops varying in length from 1.5 mi. to 3 mi. The North Trail remains in the open for almost its entire length, skirting the edges of fields and former pastureland. The Oak Loop takes you over a stream into less-disturbed forest. The west leg of the Caves Trail follows along the top of a dolostone ledge. Water flowing down from the nearby hills meets the ledge and disappears beneath it, dissolving the stone and forming caves. A spur off the north point of the Caves Trail dead-ends at a private driveway, just after passing an old cellar hole and foundation. All the trails at Field Farm are suitable for cross-country skiing.

PHELPS TRAIL
Distance: 1.9 miles to the Taconic Crest Trail
Estimated time: 1 hour
Map location: C – 13
Blazes: Blue
Maintenance: Williamstown Rural Lands Foundation, Department of Conservation and Recreation, Williamstown Conservation Commission

This trail, constructed in the 1990s, ascends a ridge jutting east from the Taconic Range, providing access to the Taconic Crest Trail.

HOW TO GET THERE
- Take Route 7 south from Williamstown to Five Corners (4.1 mi.), the junction with Route 43 (flashing light).
- Turn right on Route 43, and immediately right on Sloan Road (west).
- Go west on Sloan Road to the T-intersection with Oblong Road, and turn left (5.3 mi.).
- The trailhead is on the right (west), at a parking area marked with blue State Forest boundary tags and a large sign (5.6 mi.).

DESCRIPTION
From the trail sign (0.0 mi.), follow blue blazes west across an open field and into the woods. After crossing a fence line, enter an area of spruce and hemlock trees before the intersection with an old woods road (0.2 mi.).

Turn left onto the woods road and climb moderately into a mixed deciduous forest where the trail turns sharply to the right at the first of several switchbacks (0.3 mi.). The trail again turns sharply right to leave a woods road and climb more steeply at

0.7 miles.

At 1.0 mi., the trail crosses through a gap in the first of three old stone walls. Shortly after crossing the second stone wall, the trail rounds the shoulder of the spur, coming close to the State Forest boundary, where it turns to the right and continues upwards. (Be careful not to confuse the blazes marking the trail with the large blue paint swatches indicating the boundary line). After crossing the third stone wall (1.3 mi.), you crest the spur, and the trail levels briefly at a lookout with views of Mt. Greylock before beginning the final ascent to the **Taconic Crest Trail** (1.9 mi.).

The Taconic Crest Trail (TCT) runs north-to-south along the range crest. It is blazed with white and blue diamond tags nailed to trees along the trail. Some tags have been painted day-glow orange by snowmobile and all-terrain vehicle (ATV) users. From the Phelps Trail/TCT junction, **Berlin Mountain** is approximately 1.9 mi. to the north. 1.0 mi. to the south is the junction of the TCT, **Mills Hollow**, and Southeast Hollow Trails.

MILLS HOLLOW TRAIL
Distance: 1.6 miles
Estimated time: 1 hour
Blazes: Blue
Map location: C – 12
Maintenance: Williamstown Conservation Commission

Mills Hollow was once the only route from South Williamstown over the Taconic Range to Albany and other New York towns.

HOW TO GET THERE
- Take Route 7 south from Williamstown to Five Corners (4.1 mi.), the junction with Route 43 (flashing light).
- Turn right on Route 43, and immediately right on Sloan Road (west).
- Go west on Sloan Road to the T-intersection with Oblong Road, and turn left (5.3 mi.).
- Park at the Phelps Trail trailhead on the right (west), marked with blue State Forest boundary tags and a large sign (5.6 mi.).

- The Mills Hollow Trail starts 0.4 mi. farther along Oblong Rd (6.0 mi. total). Use the gravel road past a red gate.

DESCRIPTION

From Oblong Road the Mills Hollow Trail (0.0 mi.) begins on a grassy road a couple hundred feet south of a red gate. The gate marks the historic Mills Hollow access, now closed by an easement agreement.

Follow the grassy road across a field and into the woods; please respect the private property in this area. The road grade climbs steadily up the north side of Mills Hollow.

At 1.6 mi. you reach the **Taconic Crest Trail** (TCT) at the Massachusetts and New York state boundary. Southeast Hollow drops west into New York. A nice loop may be made with the **Phelps Trail** (4.7 mi. total) in either direction.

BENTLY HOLLOW TRAIL

Distance: 1.2 miles
Estimated time: 45 minutes
Blazes: Blue diamonds
Map location: B – 9
Maintenance: Taconic Hiking Club

The Bently Hollow trail is open for emergency use only. This is an historic route over the Taconic Range to Mattison Hollow and Cherry Plain, New York.

HOW TO GET THERE

- Take Route 7 south from Williamstown to Five Corners (4.1 mi.), the junction with Route 43 (flashing light).
- Turn right on Route 43 and drive south.
- At the Williamstown/Hancock line (7.0 mi.) be ready for a turnoff.
- 0.6 mi. beyond the town line, turn right atop a rise into what looks like a driveway. Drive a couple of hundred yards west; a sign points "To Taconic Crest Trail."
- Park off the road; do not block the private driveways.

DESCRIPTION

Walk directly west and uphill to gain the historic road grade now rutted and eroded. Scattered blue diamonds mark the route as you climb up the north side of Bently Hollow on a steep grade to the **Taconic Crest Trail**.

At the Taconic Crest you may hike north or south, but plan a car shuttle at other trailheads. The Mattison Hollow Trail, to the west, leads down into NY.

TACONIC CREST TRAIL

The Taconic Crest Trail runs 37 miles along the Taconic Range from Hancock, Massachusetts, to North Petersburg, New York, at an average elevation at 2,200 feet. Hikers, skiers, and mountain bikers share a wide, braided trail system with ATV riders, snowmobilers, and the occasional jeep.

Blue square markers, with an inset white diamond, mark the official route. You may encounter other marks, from private users and past trail surveys. Feeder trails from the east and west generally have blue diamond markers or blue painted blazes.

Access from North Berkshire includes, from north to south: Birch Brook Trail, R.R.R. Brooks and Shepherd's Well Trails, Sara Tenney Trail, Petersburg Pass, Berlin Pass Trail, Class of '33 Trail, Phelps Trail, and Mills Hollow Trail. All are described in the Taconic Range section of this guide.

During late summer, water may be difficult to find near the crest. Plan accordingly; carry extra water and be prepared for long sidehikes to fill up your water bottles.

Many organizations combine efforts to manage and protect the Taconic Trail system that also includes the South Taconic Trail: the Taconic Hiking Club, Appalachian Mountain Club, Williamstown Rural Lands Foundation, the Massachusetts Department of Conservation and Recreation, the New York Department of Environmental Conservation, and the National Park Service.

TACONIC CREST TRAIL
NORTH OF PETERSBURG PASS

Distances: 0.4 mile to Shepherd's Well Trail, 1.0 mile to Birch
     Brook Trail, 2.6 miles to Snow Hole
Estimated time: 1.5 hours to Snow Hole
Blazes: White diamonds
Map location: B – 20
Maintenance: Taconic Hiking Club

From Petersburg Pass Scenic Area a short hike accesses beautiful views along White Rocks and the spur trails of Shepherd's Well and Birch Brook. Farther north, the Snow Hole occasionally holds snow and ice well into summer.

HOW TO GET THERE
- Take Routes 7 and 2 southwest to where they split (2.3 mi.).
- Follow Route 2 west to Petersburg Pass (6.2 mi.).
- Park on the left (south) side of Route 2 at Petersburg Pass Scenic Area.

DESCRIPTION
Walk north across the highway (0.0 mi.) and up a steep bank to an open shrubby area with fine views. The trail stays west of the ridgeline until you pass the **Shepherd's Well Trail** on the right at 0.4 mile. Continue north into a large clearing with panoramic views, particularly from the knoll. This first mile of trail is known as White Rocks, named after the outcroppings of white quartz vein.

At 1.0 mi. the **Birch Brook Trail** leads east to the **Hopkins Memorial Forest Loop Trail**. Farther north, you enter Vermont and then return to New York following the ridge. At 2.6 mi. a short path forking to the right leads to the Snow Hole, a deep bedrock cleft that sometimes holds snow and ice well into summer and occasionally year-round.

Another 4.9 mi. north, and the Taconic Crest Trail ends at Route 346 in North Petersburg, NY. An alternate route leads to Prosser Hollow Road, off Route 22 in Petersburg.

TACONIC CREST TRAIL
SOUTH OF PETERSBURG PASS

Distances: 1.5 miles to Berlin Pass Trail, 2.7 miles to Berlin
Mountain, 5.2 to Mills Hollow, 8.2 miles to Bently
Hollow
Estimated time: 1.5 hours to Berlin Mountain
Blazes: White diamonds
Map location: B – 20
Maintenance: Taconic Hiking Club

Petersburg Pass Scenic Area provides a convenient access to the
Taconic Crest Trail and spur trails to the south. The views from
Berlin Mountain may be attained with a couple-hour hike. Motor-
ized vehicles have created a network of trails along the ridge. Try
to follow blazes, and stay high on the crest.

HOW TO GET THERE
- Take Routes 7 and 2 southwest to where they split (2.3 mi.).
- Follow Route 2 west up the Taconic Range to Petersburg
  Pass (6.2 mi.).
- Park on the left (south) side of Route 2 at Petersburg Pass
  Scenic Area.

DESCRIPTION
Start right (west) of the ridge (0.0 mi.) and ascend the wood road
toward the crest. You will skirt west of Mt. Raimer, where a ski
lift once served a small system of trails now growing over.

You pass through an open area (1.0 mi.) then descend to Berlin
Pass (1.5 mi.) where the **Berlin Pass Trail** joins from the left.
Continue south through alternating woods and meadow. At 2.0 mi.
an abandoned charcoal furnace lies fifty yards west of the trail. The
summit of **Berlin Mountain** affords a 360-degree view (2.7 mi.).

The Taconic Crest Trail continues southeast through a spruce
grove and then a short hardwood forest. The **Phelps Trail** enters
from the east at 4.2 mi, and at 4.7 mi. you may find water at a small
spring about 300 feet to the west of the saddle.

At 5.2 mi. you reach another saddle and the **Mills Hollow Trail**
near the New York–Massachusetts boundary. Water may be found
about 0.7 mi. to the west into Southeast Hollow.

Another 3.0 mi. south through forest and field and over several knobs leads to a saddle and the **Bently Hollow Trail**.

The Taconic Crest Trail continues 19.4 mi. south to Route 20 past Rathburn Hollow, Rounds Mountain, the Town of Hancock, Poppy Mountain, and Berry Pond. For more information refer to the *Taconic Crest Trail Guide*, a free map available from Pittsfield State Forest, the *AMC Massachusetts and Rhode Island Trail Guide,* or contact the Taconic Hiking Club.

GREYLOCK RANGE

Mt. Greylock rises over 2,500 feet above the Green and Hoosic River valleys in North Berkshire County. For centuries Greylock has drawn people for hunting, gathering, fishing, farming, grazing, timber, hydroelectric power, scientific observations, and recreation. Some say that the mountain was named for a local Indian chief, nicknamed "Gray Lock," while others contend that its name refers to the clouds that frequently sheath the summit.

Mt. Greylock offers one of the most spectacular 360-degree panoramas available, and claims the highest point in Massachusetts. A granite tower at the summit was built as a war memorial for the citizens of Massachusetts. From the observation platform near the top of the 100-foot tower you may see between 70 and 100 miles. On a clear day, it is possible to identify landmarks in five different states including: Vermont's Green Mountains to the north, New Hampshire's Mt. Monadnock to the northeast, the Catskills in New York to the west, Bear Mountain in Connecticut, and Pontoosuc and Onota Lakes in Pittsfield to the south.

Most of the Greylock Range is in the Mt. Greylock State Reservation, which was established in 1898 and contains nearly 12,000 acres. From north to south, the mountains are Mt. Prospect (2,690 feet), Mt. Williams (2,951 feet), Mt. Fitch (3,110 feet), Mt. Greylock (3,491 feet) and Saddle Ball Mountain (3,234 feet).

The Hopper, an enclosed valley named for its resemblance to a grain hopper, is on the western side of Greylock. From its base, the heavily wooded slopes rise steeply for over 1,500 feet. Designated as a National Natural Landmark in 1986, it contains a stand of old growth red spruce and beautiful cascading brooks.

Like virtually all New England mountains, old logging roads and numerous trails lace the range, including a 12 mile section of the Appalachian Trail that traverses north and south. Most of the forest is northern hardwood, but the upper slopes of Greylock and Saddle Ball, the two highest peaks, are covered with a boreal type forest of balsam fir and yellow birch, more similar to northern

Canada than the rest of New England. In addition to common wildlife like white-tailed deer, ruffed grouse, raccoon, woodchucks, and wild turkey, more than 40 state-listed rare or endangered species have been identified within the reservation.

The Department of Conservation and Recreation (DCR) maintains and manages facilities and trails in the Reservation. The Appalachian Mountain Club and Williams Outing Club also help maintain the trails. This guide includes descriptions of trails in the Reservation, roughly ordered closest-to-farthest in terms of distance from Williams College, subdivided into geographic areas: The Hopper, Greylock West, Greylock North, Greylock Summit, Greylock East, and Greylock South.

New trails may be built and old trails closed or rerouted. Each year the DCR produces a current map free to all visitors. Pick one up at Rockwell Road, Bascom Lodge at the summit, or Sperry Road Campground.

> It would be no small advantage if every college were located thus at the base of a mountain, as good at least as one well-endowed professorship...Some will remember, no doubt, not only that they went to college, but that they went to the mountain.
>
> - Henry David Thoreau
> Upon his visit to Mt. Greylock in 1844

THE HOPPER

The Hopper is so named because of its resemblance to a grain chute when viewed from vantage points to the west, such as Route 7 near South Williamstown. Several trails ascend to high points of the Greylock Range from Money and Hopper Brooks.

MONEY BROOK TRAIL

Distances: 3.1 miles to Wilbur Clearing lean-to, 3.3 miles to the Appalachian Trail, 6.8 miles to Mt. Greylock summit
Estimated time: 4.5 hours to summit
Map location: I – 12
Blazes: Blue
Maintenance: Department of Conservation and Recreation

Coupled with the Appalachian Trail, the Money Brook Trail forms a long, picturesque route to the summit of Mt. Greylock. It also forms a nice circuit with either the Hopper or Prospect Mountain Trails. For much of its length, the trail follows first Hopper Brook and then Money Brook, veering away from them only in the last mile. Money Brook is named for a band of counterfeiters who are said to have used the area as their hideout during the 1700s, and whose ghosts were later believed to haunt the surrounding woods.

HOW TO GET THERE

- From the junction of Routes 2 and 7, take Route 2 east to Route 43.
- Take Route 43 (Water St.) south to the Mt. Hope Park entrance (2.7 mi.).
- Turn left on Hopper Road. At a fork (4.1 mi.) bear left as blacktop gives way to dirt.
- At the end of the dirt road, use the designated parking on the right. There is an information board with a map of the Greylock Reservation and other information.

DESCRIPTION

Just east of the parking area (0.0 mi.), the trail begins at the entrance to an old farm road that once extended into the Hopper. Passing through a gate slightly farther ahead, the trail continues along the road between maintained fields.

After the **Hopper Trail** diverges right, the Money Brook Trail continues to follow the woods road, coming out into a level field alongside Hopper Brook.

A short way beyond the end of the field, cross Money Brook on the Bob Quay (Williams College '04) memorial bridge. As you continue along the north bank of the brook, watch for a small gorge below. Follow the trail until it reaches a second bridge over Money Brook. Cross the bridge. About 100 feet beyond, a cut-off marked with blue leads south to the Hopper Trail.

Turn left to leave the brook and ascend a hill before descending to cross a small tributary, which may be dry in late summer. Just after crossing Money Brook (1.5 mi.), the **Mt. Prospect Trail** veers off to the left.

From here the Money Brook Trail follows the stream, but never crosses it. As you gradually gain elevation above the brook, cross a small tributary (2.2 mi.) to a steeper section, eventually making a sharp left (2.5 mi.).

A side trail continues 0.1 mi. straight to Money Brook Falls, a worthwhile diversion, especially in spring. The main trail climbs steeply out of the gorge, and you quickly lose the sound of the stream. At a level section, the Money Brook Cut-off leads 0.3 mi. east to **Notch Road**.

The Money Brook Trail continues through a stand of spruce, and passes a trail leading west to the Wilbur Clearing Lean-to (3.1 mi.). This sturdy, floored shelter sleeps six people, but locating water may be a problem during the dry season. It was named for Jeremiah Wilbur, one of the original settlers in the Greylock area, who at one time farmed a 1,600-acre area stretching from **Bellows Pipe** over the top of Mt. Williams.

Just beyond the shelter, the Money Brook Trail terminates at an intersection with the **Appalachian Trail** (3.3 mi.). To the left, the AT leads up Prospect Mountain, and to the right are Notch Road and the AT route over Mts. Williams, Fitch, and Greylock.

HOPPER BROOK LOOP

Distances: 0.5 miles
Estimated time: 30 minutes
Map location: I – 13
Blazes: None
Maintenance: Department of Conservation and Recreation

This short walk in the Hopper takes you through an old pasture and near the Hopper Brook.

HOW TO GET THERE

• Refer to directions for the Money Brook Trail (page 106).

DESCRIPTION

Just east of the parking area (0.0 mi.), the trail begins at the entrance to an old farm road that once extended into the Hopper. Passing through a gate, the trail continues along the road between maintained fields.

Just after the **Haley Farm Trail** diverges on the right, you will see the Hopper Brook Loop trailhead on the left (0.2 mi.). Begin a descent northward, keeping to your left a fine example of an old stone wall. Turn right (0.3 mi.) to continue your descent. Note the abundance of Japanese barberry on the forest floor beneath a canopy of maples and birch trees. There are also a few apple trees scattered throughout. After another right turn (0.4 mi.), the trail takes you south and across a small stream via a footbridge. Soon after, you arrive at a small clearing. To the left you can hear, and walk a few steps to reach, the Hopper Brook. Continue along the trail and arrive at a T-junction with the **Money Brook Trail** (0.6 mi.). Turn right to return to the parking lot along the original old farm road (1.0 mi.). Or, for a longer hike, turn left onto the Money Brook Trail.

HALEY FARM TRAIL

Distance: 2.2 miles to Stony Ledge
Estimated time: 2.0 hours
Map location: I – 12
Blazes: Blue
Maintenance: Department of Conservation and Recreation

Haley and Greene farms have been active in the Hopper for centuries. The Commonwealth of Massachusetts, through the Department of Environmental Management (now DCR), bought this land with the help of the Williamstown Rural Lands Foundation to protect access to the Hopper and Mt. Greylock Reservation in 1990. In 1997, the DEM cut the Haley Farm Trail to provide a new short, steep route to Stony Ledge.

HOW TO GET THERE

• Refer to directions for the Money Brook Trail (page 106).

DESCRIPTION

Just east of the parking area (0.0 mi.), the trail begins at the entrance to an old farm road that once extended into the Hopper. The trail continues on this road, passing through a gate slightly farther on, and then between maintained fields.

The Haley Farm Trail leaves to the right (south). The **Money Brook Trail** and **Hopper Trail** continue straight ahead. From the stone wall (0.0 mi.), cross a field due south toward the treeline along a sparsely marked path.

Enter the trees, and bear right to begin a gentle ascent. The open forest is dominated by tall, thin red maples, suggesting the recent history of agriculture. At the first of a series of switchbacks, the trail begins to climb much more steeply, broken up somewhat by a number of level stretches until the top of the east-west ridge is reached.

As you gain elevation the grade gradually eases through a large grove of juvenile birch and striped maple. After scrambling through and out of an old rocky gully – and passing a cut-out view of Williamstown to the north – you join the **Stony Ledge Trail** (1.8 mi.) for one final climb past the Stony Ledge shelter and campsite.

Finally, a breathtaking view from Stony Ledge rewards your perseverance. On a clear day it is possible to look down into the Hopper and up to the summits of Mts. Greylock, Fitch, and Williams to the east. Prospect Mountain defines the opposite edge of the Hopper to the north.

HOPPER TRAIL

Distances: 2.4 miles to Sperry Road, 4.1 mi. to Greylock summit
Estimated time: 2.5 hours to summit
Map location: I – 12
Blazes: Blue
Maintenance: Department of Conservation and Recreation

On May 12, 1830, a group of over 100 people — a majority of them Williams students and faculty — left Haley's farm at the mouth of the Hopper and cleared a road to the summit of Mt. Greylock (according to "The American Advocate," a Williamstown newspaper of the day). The long history and direct route of the Hopper Trail make it one of the most hiked trails in the Mt. Greylock Reservation.

HOW TO GET THERE
• Refer to directions for the Money Brook Trail (page 106).

DESCRIPTION
Just east of the parking area (0.0 mi.), the trail begins at the entrance to an old farm road that once extended into the Hopper. The trail continues on this road, passing through a gate slightly farther on, and then between maintained fields.

The **Haley Farm Trail** diverges to the right. After another 100 yards, the Hopper Trail also bears off to the right, as the **Money Brook Trail** continues straight down the hill.

The Hopper Trail ascends through an overgrown pasture, scattered with wildflowers and a handful of twisted old apple trees. Enter the woods at the southeast corner of the field, and climb gently through an open forest. Through the trees to the left you can hear Hopper Brook, which cascades along the bottom of the valley, out of sight. At 1.5 mi., pass a cut-off heading north to the Money Brook Trail.

The ascent steepens and you pass through an extensive grove of young trees before gradually leveling out in a red spruce forest near **Sperry Road** in the middle of the campground (2.4 mi.).

Turn left and walk southeast along Sperry Road and around a bend to the right (south). Look for the Hopper Trail to the left, just after passing the campground office, heading east to the Mt. Greylock summit. The trail arrives at a T-intersection with the original carriage road to the summit from the south. To the right is an extension of the **Deer Hill Trail**. The Hopper Trail takes a left onto the woods road, crosses a stream – the beginning of Roaring Brook – and enters a spruce grove.

Continue upward and cross two small streams. At a sharp right turn, the **Overlook Trail** descends to the left. Stay on the Hopper Trail; it will soon parallel **Rockwell Road**. The trail ends at its intersection with the **Appalachian Trail** (AT) (3.2 mi.). Follow the AT to the Mt. Greylock summit (3.9 mi.).

MT. PROSPECT TRAIL

Distance: 4.0 miles to Appalachian Trail from Hopper trail-head
Estimated time: 3 hours
Map location: K – 12
Blazes: Blue
Maintenance: Department of Conservation and Recreation

The Mt. Prospect Trail is one of the most difficult hikes in the Greylock Reservation, but it is also one of the most beautiful. It offers breathtaking views of the Hopper, the "Purple Valley," and the Taconic Range. Together with the Appalachian and Money Brook Trails, it makes an attractive 7.8 mi. loop.

HOW TO GET THERE
  • Refer to directions for the Money Brook Trail (page 106).

DESCRIPTION
Take the **Money Brook Trail** from Haley's Farm. 1.7 mi. from

the trailhead, just after it crosses Money Brook for the last time, the Mt. Prospect Trail diverges to the left.

Leave the Money Brook Trail and climb gradually up the northeast side of the ravine to the sharp ridge of Prospect Mountain (2.2 mi.), which it follows to the summit (3.0 mi.). The steepness of this section of the trail is compensated for by overlooks with spectacular views of the Hopper, on the western side of Mt. Greylock. Look for the large groves of red spruce about halfway up The Hopper—these stands of 200-year-old trees were designated a Natural National Landmark in 1987.

Although there is no view from the top of Mt. Prospect (2,690 feet), a rock cairn marking the summit lets you know your climb is at its end. The trail winds north along the ridge, through a forest of red maple, beech, and yellow birch. The trail ultimately joins the **Appalachian Trail** (4.0 mi.).

The "Prospect Lookout" at the junction is one of the best views in the Greylock Range. The valleys of the **Green River** and **Hoosic River** unfold to the west, at the base of the **Taconic Range**, and the **Green Mountains** of Vermont rise to the northwest. In spring and fall, this is also an excellent place to watch migrating hawks sail past.

To return to the Haley Farm, follow the Appalachian Trail to the right (southeast). After 0.3 mi. turn right on the Money Brook Trail and follow it to the Hopper Trailhead (7.8 mi.).

GREYLOCK NORTH

Mt. Prospect and Mt. Williams rise prominently above Williamstown and the Hoosic River. The Appalachian Trail and several other trails climb this northern end of the Greylock Range a few miles southeast of Williams College.

APPALACHIAN TRAIL
PATTISON ROAD TO MT. GREYLOCK

Distance: 5.2 miles to Mt. Greylock summit
Estimated time: 3 hours
Map location: L – 16
Blazes: White
Maintenance: AMC Mass. AT Committee

Be prepared from the start for a steep climb up Mt. Prospect, one of the steepest in the region. This route touches on some of the major peaks of the Greylock Range: Mt. Williams (2,951 feet), Mt. Fitch (3,110 feet) and Mt. Greylock (3,491 feet).

HOW TO GET THERE
- From the junction of Routes 2 and 7, take Route 2 east towards North Adams.
- Turn right on Luce Road (1.4 mi.).
- Follow Luce Rd. past the steep dikes of the Williamstown reservoir (2.8 mi.).
- Crossing the North Adams border, the road changes from Luce to Pattison.
- The AT crosses the road 0.4 mi. beyond the reservoir. A pullout on the left allows parking for five to six vehicles.

DESCRIPTION
From Pattison Rd. (0.0 mi.), the southbound AT winds through a stand of Norway spruce planted to stabilize land on the North

Adams watershed and ascends a ridge of Mt. Prospect with many stairs and switchbacks on the north slope of Mt. Prospect (0.4 mi.), becoming quite steep near the top. When you crest the ridge (1.5 mi.), it intersects the **Mt. Prospect Trail**, which continues straight ahead while the AT turns left. From here, enjoy the precipitous view of Williamstown and the Pownal valley to the west.

Turn sharply left (east) towards Mt. Williams on the AT (white blazes). The trail leaves Mt. Prospect Ridge and descends to meet the **Money Brook Trail** in a grove of towering red spruce, some as much as 130 years old. The Wilbur Clearing Shelter (which sleeps six people), five tent platforms, and two tent pads are located at a campsite 0.3 mi. south along the Money Brook Trail.

Continuing south on the AT, beyond the Money Brook Trail, is a junction with a blue-blazed side trail to the right leading to day-use parking at **Notch Road**. Shortly after this junction, the AT crosses Notch Road 100 yards from the parking area. The next junction (also to the right) is the northern end of the **Old Summit Road** (which also leads back to the Notch Road parking area and then continues south and east to rejoin the AT south of Mt. Williams). Old Summit Road can be used to bypass the climb to the summit of Mt. Williams, if desired.

Continue hiking south on the AT and ascend Mt. Williams, making several sharp turns and scrambling up short rock outcroppings. From the summit (2.7 mi.), there are obscured views to the east and north. At the summit, the AT turns sharply right (south) and descends to a junction with the **Bernard Farm Trail** (east) and Old Summit Road (which leads west, then north to the previously mentioned day-use parking area on Notch Road.) An obscure granite town boundary marker may be found in the woods to the right (west) of the AT near this junction. This is easiest to spot when the leaves are down.

From the Mt. Williams summit, descend to a saddle (3.1 mi.). Cross an unusual outcropping of milky quartz, then come to an open, east-facing junction with the **Bellows Pipe Trail**. Just beyond this junction (within 100 yards), the **Thunderbolt Trail** (3.3 mi.). Both trails descend steeply east to the Bellows Pipe Trail and eventually **Greylock Glen**.

The AT begins to climb, and another side trail to Notch Road (in 0.2 mi.) and **Robinson Point Trail** appears on the right. The AT then climbs steeply and crosses Summit Road. Continuing steeply, the end of the Mt. Greylock summit parking lot is reached, and the enclosed Thunderbolt shelter is on the right (not for overnight use). To reach the summit of Mt. Greylock, continue on the AT past the shelter (5.2 mi.).

NOTCH ROAD
Distances: 8.4 miles to Rockwell Road, 9.1 miles to summit
Estimated time: 30 minutes driving
Map location: N – 17
Blazes: None
Maintenance: Department of Conservation and Recreation

The former Braytonville Carriage Road is a hard-surfaced road that provides auto access to Greylock's summit during the summer months. It can be used to reach the Money Brook, Overlook, Bellows Pipe, Bernard Farm, Robinson's Point, and Appalachian Trails, as well as the Old Summit Road. During the winter, snowmobiles and cross-country skiers use the road.

HOW TO GET THERE
• From Field Park follow Route 2 east to Braytonville.
• After the second Hoosic River crossing, turn right on Notch Road (4.1 mi.).

DESCRIPTION
From Route 2 (0.0 mi.), Notch Road travels south to the intersection with Pattison Road, where it makes a sharp left (1.3 mi.) at the Mt. Williams Reservoir. Pass through dense pine and Norway spruce forest and then open fields to reach an intersection with Reservoir Road near several houses at the base of Mt. Williams (2.4 mi.). From this junction, the **Bellows Pipe Trail** goes straight. Notch Road continues to the west (right).

As you enter the Greylock Reservation (3.0 mi.) the **Bernard Farm Trail** starts to the north out of the parking lot, and Notch Road switchbacks up to a low point in the saddle between Mt. Williams and Mt. Prospect. Here, you intersect the **Appalachian Trail** (4.4 mi.). Limited day-parking is available at this crossing. Continue the ascent past the Money Brook Cut-off (5.1 mi.), a

0.2 mi. shortcut which connects with the **Money Brook Trail**. At the point where Notch Road crosses Money Brook, a 0.2 mi. access trail leads east to the Appalachian Trail (AT).

The upper section of Notch Road offers several impressive views of the Hopper. Just south of the **Robinson's Point Trail**, there is a pullout on the west side of the road (7.4 mi.), across from a second cutoff to the AT. Slightly south of the pullout is the road-crossing of the **Overlook Trail** (7.5 mi.).

Notch Road continues to another AT crossing (8.4 mi.), where it intersects **Rockwell Road** and **Summit Road** at yet another AT crossing. Summit Road spirals the final distance up Greylock (9.1 mi.).

CASCADES TRAIL

Distance: 1.0 mile (round-trip)
Estimated time: 45 minutes
Blazes: None
Map location: N – 17
Maintenance: Town of North Adams, Berkshire Natural Resources Council

Hidden in the middle of development, the Cascades is a beautiful waterfall in North Adams along Notch Brook.

HOW TO GET THERE

- From Field Park follow Route 2 east to North Adams.
- After the second Hoosic River crossing, turn right at Brayton Hill Terrace and bear left up the hill to Brayton Elementary School and YMCA (4.0 mi.).
- Behind the school, park at the trailhead kiosk and follow the trail across the bridge and into the Marion Avenue neighborhood. Parking is not permitted on Marion Ave.

DESCRIPTION

The Cascades Trail is an extension of Marion Avenue. You follow Notch Brook and cross it a couple of times. The Cascades (0.5 mi.) plunge about fifty feet where harder rock has eroded more slowly than the marble downstream. Notch brook originates in the **Bellows Pipe** between **Ragged Mountain** and Mt. Williams. Return the way you came (1.0 mi.).

BERNARD FARM TRAIL

Distance: 2.3 miles (approximately) to Appalachian Trail
Estimated time: 2 hours
Blazes: Blue
Map location: N – 15
Maintenance: Department of Conservation and Recreation

From Bernard Farm, this trail connects a series of woods roads alongside Notch Road up the flank of Mt. Williams. It offers a direct route to the Appalachian Trail (AT) and the summit of Greylock.

HOW TO GET THERE
- From Field Park follow Route 2 east.
- After the second Hoosic River crossing, turn right on Notch Road (4.1 mi.).
- At an intersection by Mt. Williams Reservoir, follow Notch Rd. to the left (east) (5.3 mi.).
- At the next intersection, Notch Road turns right and continues uphill to the Mt. Greylock Reservation Parking area, which is open year-round (6.5 mi.).

DESCRIPTION
Harry Bernard ran a dairy farm on this site in the early part of the 20th century. He also drove children to school with his "school team" before buses, extracted timber used for construction of Bascom Lodge in the 1930s, and operated a small ski area in the 1940s and 1950s.

The trail initially leads west and south from the parking area and follows a series of trails and woods roads up the mountainside. After crossing **Notch Road**, the trail turns west to join an historic road before heading south within sight of one of Notch Road's switchbacks. Pass a granite boundary marker and continue south for 0.5 mi. Here, the trail leaves the road and heads west, switching-back up Mt. Williams (paralleling the North Adams watershed boundary) before then leading south. The trail passes the remains of an old airplane after crossing into the North Adams watershed, and meets the **Appalachian Trail** just south of Mt. Williams (2.3 mi.).

BELLOWS PIPE TRAIL

Distance: 4.5 miles
Estimated time: 3.0 hours
Blazes: Blue
Map location: N – 14
Maintenance: Department of Conservation and Recreation

Bellows Pipe, named for the roar of wind in this tight valley, was originally called the Notch; a name still held by the stream that flows down it and the road that accesses the area. Jeremiah Wilbur cleared a road up the Notch and on to the summit of Greylock in the late 18th Century. The Bellows Pipe Trail follows portions of this old route, and offers access to Ragged Mountain.

HOW TO GET THERE
- Drive east on Route 2 from Routes 2 and 7 in Williamstown.
- After crossing the Hoosic for the second time, turn right (south) on Notch Road (4.1 mi.).
- At an intersection by Mt. Williams Reservoir, follow Notch Rd. to the left (east) (5.3 mi.).
- At the next intersection, Notch Road turns right and continues uphill to the Mt. Greylock Reservation Parking area, which is open year-round (6.5 mi.).

DESCRIPTION
The trail follows an old woods road, maybe the route of Jeremiah Wilbur's original summit road. As you climb along Notch Brook, imagine an active farm with three mills along the brook, hay fields, gardens, orchards, a stand of sugar maple, cows, and sheep.

At 2.2 mi. you reach the saddle between **Ragged Mountain** and Greylock's northeastern slope. Here a short trail to the left (east) leads to Ragged Mountain.

At a trail junction (2.5 mi.), an old road intersects straight ahead with the **Thunderbolt Trail** and drops to the Gould Farm. Turn right to reach the Bellows Pipe Shelter before coming to steeper terrain with a series of switchbacks to the **Appalachian Trail** (AT) marked by white blazes.

Turn left on the AT, pass the top of the Thunderbolt Trail, and climb steeply towards the summit. Cross the **Summit Road** just before the summit clearing and War Memorial (4.5 mi.).

RAGGED MOUNTAIN TRAIL

Distance: 0.4 mile (approximately)
Estimated time: 20 minutes
Blazes: Blue
Map location: M – 11
Maintenance: Department of Conservation and Recreation

This short spur trail ascends to the summit of Ragged Mountain from the Bellows Pipe, also known as the Notch. In 1910 the Massachusetts State legislature authorized a trolley line from Adams to this point and onto the summit of Greylock. Three years later the proposal died.

HOW TO GET THERE

- Ascend the Bellows Pipe Trail or Thunderbolt Trail to the saddle between Ragged Mountain and Mt. Greylock.
- Alternatively, descend the Appalachian Trail and Bellows Pipe Trail from the summit of Greylock.

DESCRIPTION

From the **Bellows Pipe Trail** (0.0 mi.): in the saddle, follow a spur trail to the east. You climb a winding, steep route to the summit of Ragged Mountain in about twenty minutes (0.4 mi.). From here are excellent views south to Mt. Greylock, Saddle Ball Mountain and Greylock Glen.

OLD SUMMIT ROAD

Distance: 0.8 mile (approximately)
Estimated time: 25 minutes
Blazes: Blue
Map location: L – 14
Maintenance: Department of Conservation and Recreation

Named for a historic road up Greylock, this trail bypasses the summit of Mt. Williams between sections of Notch Road and the Appalachian Trail.

HOW TO GET THERE

- Most will use this trail as a convenient cut-off when hiking the Appalachian Trail (AT).
- By car: refer to directions and description for Notch Road. Park at the AT crossing 1.4 mi. from the Reservation boundary.

DESCRIPTION

Head east from the **Appalachian Trail** day-use parking area. Along the way you will pass signed cut-offs to the AT, **Notch Road** and **Money Brook Trail**. One-quarter mile before the junction with the AT and **Bernard Farm Trail**, a chimney marks the site of the Williams Outing Club Harris Memorial Cabin built in 1932 – and burned mysteriously on Halloween night in 1961.

GREYLOCK WEST

South of the Hopper, a couple of trails climb Goodell Hollow to Sperry Road on Stony Ledge. From there, several short trails visit the cascades of March Cataract Falls and the Heart of Greylock.

ROARING BROOK TRAIL

Distance: 1.9 miles
Estimated time: 1.5 hours
Map location: H – 10
Blazes: Blue
Maintenance: Department of Conservation and Recreation

The Roaring Brook and Stony Ledge Trails form an excellent five-mile loop to views of the Hopper and Greylock Range from Stony Ledge. Many prefer to hike up the steep Stony Ledge Trail and descend the more gradual Roaring Brook Trail. You may also use either trail to reach the summit of Greylock and other trails in the park.

HOW TO GET THERE

- Take Route 7 south from Field Park in Williamstown.
- 1.6 mi. after the junction with Route 43 in South Williamstown, turn left on Roaring Brook Road (5.7 mi. total).
- Drive 0.5 mi. to a sign for the Mt. Greylock Ski Club and a pullout on the left. The road is private beyond this point, so all cars should be parked here.

DESCRIPTION

Start on the woods road to the left, along Roaring Brook (0.0 mi.). Cross Roaring Brook via a footbridge, ascend slightly, and then descend to cross the brook again on another bridge. Proceed through the meadow on the south side of the stream, bear left at a split in the dirt road and make a third crossing of Roaring Brook. This third crossing must be made without the aid of a bridge. Take care while crossing: use your judgement to determine whether the crossing can be made safely depending on the water conditions and your physical ability.

At 0.5 mi. the Roaring Brook Trail and **Stony Ledge Trail** diverge on the north side of Roaring Brook. From here, you leave the brook and rapidly ascend through a mixture of evergreen and deciduous trees to a hemlock grove, where the grade finally flattens out (1.6 mi.).

Just before a bridge over Roaring Brook (1.8 mi.), the **Deer Hill Trail** leaves to the right. Continue parallel to the brook for another 200 yards and enter Sperry Campground. There are picnic tables, campsites, and group shelters (fee and reservation) here.

Turn left (north) and cross a bridge over Roaring Brook. The Roaring Brook Trail follows the campground road to intersect with Sperry Road (1.9 mi.) and the **Hopper Trail**. The summit of Greylock is 2.3 mi. east along the Hopper Trail (4.2 mi. total).

For a spectacular view of the entire Greylock Reservation, turn left (west) on Sperry Road and walk 1.0 mi. up to the Stony Ledge picnic area (3.0 mi.). Straight across from the ledge (east) is the Greylock summit, and to the left are Mt. Fitch, Mt. Williams, and Mt. Prospect. Stony Ledge is the site of **Mountain Day**, the Williams Outing Club's annual celebration of the fall foliage.

You can return to Roaring Brook Road via the Stony Ledge Trail (5.1 mi.), but it is a much steeper descent than the Roaring Brook Trail. Otherwise, retrace your steps, or continue over the range to a car shuttle.

STONY LEDGE TRAIL

Distance: 2.1 miles
Estimated time: 1.5 hours
Map location: H – 10
Blazes: Blue
Maintenance: Department of Conservation and Recreation

The Civilian Conservation Corps (CCC) and the Mt. Greylock Ski Club built the Stony Ledge Ski Trail in the 1930s, but it has not been maintained for skiing recently. This steep climb ends with magnificent views across the Hopper from Stony Ledge. Descend the Roaring Brook Trail for a 5.1-mile loop.

HOW TO GET THERE
• Refer to directions for the Roaring Brook Trail (page 121).

DESCRIPTION
Start on the woods road to the left, along Roaring Brook (0.0 mi.). You cross Roaring Brook, ascend slightly, and then descend to cross the brook again. Proceed through the meadow on the south side of the stream, bear left at a split in the dirt road and make a third crossing of Roaring Brook.

At 0.5 mi., the **Roaring Brook Trail** and Stony Ledge Trail diverge on the north side of Roaring Brook. Follow an old woods road on a gradual climb to the north. At 1.2 mi., the trail swings right (east) onto the steep part of the old ski trail.

You crest the ridge near a lean-to and continue to the lookout from Stony Ledge (2.1 mi.). Here you can see (from left to right) **Prospect Mountain**, Mt. Williams, Mt. Fitch, Mt. Greylock, and part of Saddle Ball Mountain.

SPERRY ROAD
Distance: 1.7 miles to Stony Ledge
Estimated time: 1 hour
Blazes: None
Map location: J – 9
Maintenance: Department of Conservation and Recreation

Sperry Road provides access to Sperry Campground, Stony Ledge, and several trails from Rockwell Road. The Civilian Conservation Corps based its Greylock crew here in the 1930s.

HOW TO GET THERE
• Refer to description for Rockwell Road.
• Sperry Road leaves Rockwell Road 6.3 mi. from Quarry Road.

DESCRIPTION
Sperry Road leads 0.6 mi. to Sperry Campground and 1.7 mi. to Stony Ledge. Sperry Campground was a farm site in the late 1700s. In 1863, the Williams Alpine Club established a camping area there. Later, the Civilian Conservation Corps based its op-

erations and 200 men at the same site. Currently, there is no auto access onto the road.

Parking is at the junction with Rockwell Road and provides access to the **Hopper Trail**, **March Cataract Trail**, **Deer Hill Trail**, and **Roaring Brook Trail**. Sperry Road ends on the summit of Stony Ledge, just south of a shelter and the **Stony Ledge Trail**, with a view that encompasses the entire Greylock Range.

DEER HILL TRAIL

Distance: 2.0 miles (loop)
Estimated time: 1 hour 15 minutes
Blazes: Blue
Map location: J – 10
Maintenance: Department of Conservation and Recreation

This pleasant but steep loop, high on Mt. Greylock, starts and ends at Sperry Campground. Along the way are Deer Hill Falls, a shelter, and an old carriage road. The Civilian Conservation Corps built this trail to what Williams College professor Albert Hopkins called the "Heart of Greylock," a stand of old growth hemlock and red spruce at the falls.

HOW TO GET THERE

- Go to Sperry Campground. On foot, the Hopper and Roaring Brook Trail provide the most direct access. By car, use Notch Road or Rockwell Road to Sperry Road, all described in this book.
- The Deer Hill Trail begins with the Roaring Brook Trail off Sperry Road near the group fee shelters and entry station at the southeast end of the campground.

DESCRIPTION

Start on the **Roaring Brook Trail** heading southwest from Sperry Road (0.0 mi.). Soon you leave the Roaring Brook Trail (0.1 mi.) and descend to Deer Hill Falls before a greater climb up past a shelter (0.8 mi.) towards **Rockwell Road** (southeast). Turn left on a carriage road and left again on Sperry Road to return to the trailhead (2.0 mi.).

MARCH CATARACT TRAIL

Distance: 0.8 miles from Sperry Campground to falls
Estimated time: 25 minutes (one-way)
Blazes: Blue
Map location: J – 10
Maintenance: Department of Conservation and Recreation

For a short hike from Sperry Campground, try the March Cataract Trail to Bacon Brook, a tributary of Hopper Brook.

HOW TO GET THERE

- Go to Sperry Campground. On foot, the Hopper and Roaring Brook Trail provide the most direct access, although any trail to the summit area of Greylock will do. By car, use Notch Road or Rockwell Road to Sperry Road, all described in this book.
- March Cataract Trail begins at a bend in Sperry Road near the group fee shelters and entry station at the east end of the campground.

DESCRIPTION

From **Sperry Road** (0.0 mi.), follow the trail gradually up and then more steeply down into the upper reaches of the Hopper. Farther north on this steep terrain are areas of old-growth forest spared by their inaccessibility. At 0.8 mi., you reach March Cataract Falls on the upper reaches of Bacon Brook. Spring is the best time to see the cascades, when snowmelt and swollen groundwater supplies run down the mountain. Watch out for slippery, wet rocks, and ice from the spray. Return the way you came.

Greylock Range – View from North atop Pine Cobble.

GREYLOCK SUMMIT

Trails from all around converge at the 3,491' summit of Mt. Greylock. The Overlook and Robinson Point Trails provide a tour of the summit area with fantastic viewpoints. Bascom Lodge and the War Memorial offer visitor facilities for hikers and tourists.

OVERLOOK TRAIL

Distance: Part of a 2.7 mile loop from the Mt. Greylock summit
Estimated time: 1.5 hours
Map location: L – 11
Blazes: Blue
Maintenance: Department of Conservation and Recreation

Bypassing the summit of Mt. Greylock, this trail connects the Hopper Trail on the south with the Appalachian Trail on the north. On a clear day, it affords a view of the Hopper that is not possible from any other trail or summit. Link the Overlook, Hopper, and Appalachian Trails and the Old Carriage Road to make a pleasant 2.7 mile circuit from the Greylock summit. Although the trail is not steep, portions of it do require scrambling over tree roots and rocks.

HOW TO GET THERE

- You must be in the summit area of Mt. Greylock for this trail. Use any of the hiking trails from surrounding valleys, Notch Road, or Rockwell Road to ascend the mountain.
- Park at the summit or the first two day-use parking areas along Rockwell Road. The description starts from the summit of Greylock, but you may pick up the loop anywhere along the way.

DESCRIPTION

Start at the Mt. Greylock parking lot and descend the Old Carriage Road. The road starts at the southwest corner of the Radio Tower building near the exit, but the sign is only visible if you are facing south on the AT. After 0.5 mi. the trail makes a sharp left to meet and cross **Notch Road**.

From Notch Road, the trail levels out and follows the contours of the mountain. You pass through a stand of conifers, and after crossing a stream and a swampy area forested with balsam and hemlock, the trail approaches an overlook down a short side trail to the right. **Stony Ledge** is visible to the left, the south side of **Prospect Mountain** to the right, and the **Taconic Range** in the distance.

Somewhat farther on, the trail crosses Bacon Brook upstream of **March Cataract Falls**. Climb back up to the Hopper Trail and **Rockwell Road** (1.7 mi.). To return to the Greylock summit, follow the **Hopper Trail** east (left) to Rockwell Road. Join the AT where it intersects Rockwell Road (2.1 mi.), and follow it northeast to the Greylock parking lot (2.7 mi.). To reach Sperry Campground, Stony Ledge and the **Roaring Brook** trailhead, follow the Hopper Trail down to the right.

ROBINSON POINT TRAIL

Distance: 0.2 mile
Estimated time: 5-10 minutes
Blazes: Blue
Map location: L – 11
Maintenance: Department of Conservation and Recreation

A fantastic view west into the Hopper and across to the Taconic Range may be had with a short walk from Notch Road.

HOW TO GET THERE

- Refer to directions for Notch Road (page 115). 7.4 mi. from Route 2, or 4.4 mi. from the Reservation entrance, park in a pullout on the right (west side of the road).

DESCRIPTION

Follow the short, but very steep, trail down to a spectacular overlook above the Hopper. To the right is Prospect Mountain; to the left is Stony Ledge.

BASCOM LODGE

After a summit log cabin burned in 1929, the State of Massachusetts, Berkshire County, and the Civilian Conservation Corps built the more grand Bascom Lodge to match summit houses on other New England Peaks. Completed in 1937, it is constructed of native stone and timber with lodging, a dining room, staff quarters, a common room and a trading post (*Most Excellent Majesty*).

The lodge is open seasonally (May–October), and offers group and private rooms for overnight lodging. Additionally: breakfast, lunch, and dinner are served seven days per week, though reservations are required for dinner.

WAR MEMORIAL

As plans for Bascom Lodge took shape, the form of a new tower rose on Mt. Greylock where an old iron structure and the original wooden towers had stood before. The 100-foot tall granite memorial was built to honor Massachusetts men and women who died in World War I. Originally designed to be a lighthouse memorial in Boston Harbor, the structure was built instead on the summit in the 1930s. At that time, twelve powerful searchlights made the tower a beacon visible for seventy miles! Over time, the fierce mountain weather has necessitated several major repairs of the tower, most recently for the Mt. Greylock State Reservation centennial in 1998, and again in 2016. From an observation area high in the tower, you can see for over one hundred miles on a clear day.

GREYLOCK EAST

From the Town of Adams, a number of trails climb the steep east side of Mt. Greylock from Greylock Glen.

CHESHIRE HARBOR TRAIL
Distances: 2.6 miles to Rockwell Road, 3.3 miles to summit
Estimated time: 2 hours to summit
Map location: M – 7
Blazes: Blue
Maintenance: Department of Conservation and Recreation, Adams Sno-Drifters Snowmobile Club

This trail is the easiest, most direct route to the summit of Greylock, in part because it begins at a relatively high elevation. Every Columbus Day, hundreds of hikers ascend this way during the Greylock Ramble, an event sponsored by the Adams Chamber of Commerce. The trail is named for a historic town site where Basset Brook meets modern Route 8. Although it suggests proximity to a large body of water, the name actually refers to the fact that it is reported to have been a stop on the underground railroad.

HOW TO GET THERE
- Drive east on Route 2 from Williamstown.
- As you enter North Adams (5.0 mi.) follow signs to Down town, Route 8 south, and Heritage State Park; bear right to Main Street and a stop light.
- Take Route 8 south (5.1 mi.).
- At the Monument to President McKinley in Adams, turn right (west) onto Maple St. (10.4 mi.).
- Pass a cemetery and turn left. on West Road (10.8 mi.).
- After another 0.5 mi., turn right on West Mountain Road (11.3 mi. total) at a sign for Greylock Greenhouses.
- Follow for 1.6 mi. to a dead-end at the trailhead, clearly marked with a sign (12.9 mi.).

DESCRIPTION

This wide and easy-to-follow trail climbs steadily up an old woods road, passing several old stone foundations. At the first switchback, it intersects a trail to the **Gould Trail** trailhead (0.4 mi.). After two more switchbacks, the Cheshire Harbor Trail diverges from the woods road (1.0 mi.), bearing off to the right and up while the woods road bears left, becoming **Old Adams Road**.

Old Adams Road connects to the **Appalachian Trail** (AT) in approximately 1.7 miles. On a clear day, the summit of Mt. Greylock should become visible as you ascend, with the memorial tower rising over Peck's Brook ravine.

The Cheshire Harbor Trail continues to the northwest, through stands of northern hardwoods that have been severely stressed by atmospheric pollution. Scientists have designated several plots in the area to study the decline of high altitude forests in New England, and the number of dead trees suggests that the problem may be quite serious.

Just after the trail crosses Peck's Brook (2.3 mi.), it terminates at **Rockwell Road** (2.6 mi.), also the junction with the AT. From here, the summit of Mt. Greylock is 0.7 mi. north along the AT.

OLD ADAMS ROAD

Distances: 2.8 miles, Cheshire Harbor Trail to Appalachian Trail, 4.8 miles to Rockwell Road
Estimated time: 1.5 hours to Appalachian Trail
Map location: L – 8
Blazes: Blue
Maintenance: Department of Conservation and Recreation, Adams Sno-Drifters Snowmobile Club

Old Adams Road connects the Cheshire Harbor Trail, Appalachian Trail, and Rockwell Road on the southeast side of the Greylock range. It follows a near-level grade around Saddle Ball Mountain.

HOW TO GET THERE

- Refer to directions for the Cheshire Harbor Trail (page 130).
- Follow the Cheshire Harbor Trail for 1.0 mi. to the third switchback and then bear left (south) onto a woods road.

DESCRIPTION

After leaving the **Cheshire Harbor Trail** (0.0 mi.), Old Adams Road heads east, crossing a bridge over the first of a series of brooks (0.2 mi.). The bridge over the second brook (0.8 mi.) is at the base of an attractive waterfall.

Continue past a lesser-used woods road that branches left toward Cheshire (1.7 mi.), and then cross three more brooks. At the next intersection (2.7 mi.), **Redgate Road** drops to the southeast. Old Adams Road continues west to an intersection with the **Appalachian Trail** (2.8 mi.). Kitchen Brook is just west of the junction.

Old Adams Road continues another 2.0 mi. around the south end of Saddle Ball Mountain to **Rockwell Road** at the **Jones' Nose** parking area (4.8 mi.).

GOULD TRAIL

Distances: 3.0 miles to Rockwell Road, 3.4 miles to summit
Estimated time: 2.5 hours
Blazes: Blue
Map location: M – 8
Maintenance: Department of Conservation and Recreation

One of several trails from the Adams side of Greylock, the Gould Trail climbs about 1700 feet of elevation in three miles. Along the way is Peck's Brook Shelter, a beautiful spot to spend a night on Mt. Greylock.

HOW TO GET THERE

- Drive east on Route 2 from Williamstown.
- As you enter North Adams (5.0 mi.) follow signs to Down town, Route 8 south, and Heritage State Park; bear right to Main Street and a stop light.
- Take Route 8 south (5.1 mi.).
- At the Monument to President McKinley in Adams, turn right (west) onto Maple St. (10.4 mi.).
- Pass a cemetery and turn left on West Road (10.8 mi.).
- After another 0.5 mi., turn right on West Mountain Road (11.3 total) at a sign for Greylock Greenhouses.
- Follow for 0.9 mi. to a trailhead on the right, clearly marked

with a sign (12.2 mi.).

DESCRIPTION

From West Mountain Road (0.0 mi.), enter the woods at the south end of the field. At the first junction head north (right); on the left, a trail links up with the **Cheshire Harbor Trail**. After crossing Peck's Brook Bridge, a short, gradual ascent brings you to a second junction. Turn left (west) and begin your climb in earnest.

You ascend just north of Peck's Brook to a cut-off to the Cheshire Harbor Trail south of the brook. At 2.0 mi. a short side trail leads to Peck's Brook Shelter along the stream. Another mi. of steady climbing brings you to **Rockwell Road** (3.0 mi.). From the intersection of Notch and Rockwell Roads follow the **Appalachian Trail** to the summit (3.4 mi.).

REDGATE ROAD

Distance: 2.2 miles (approximately)
Estimated time: 1.5 hours
Blazes: Blue
Map location: M – 7
Maintenance: Department of Conservation and Recreation, Adams Sno-Drifters Snowmobile Club

Many trails in the North Berkshire area utilize old woods roads or turnpikes. Redgate Road is one, in places deeply gullied from use as a route from Adams to New Ashford and Lanesboro in the 1800s.

HOW TO GET THERE

• Refer to directions for the Cheshire Harbor Trail (page 130).

DESCRIPTION

From the **Cheshire Harbor Trail** trailhead, follow the abandoned continuation of West Mountain Road. After about 0.4 mi., the Redgate Road leaves to the right (west), just before Bassett Brook. The grade is obvious and a single blaze has been chopped in the bark of a sixteen-inch tree.

Soon you will cross a bridge, then turn left (southeast), off a woods road to cross another bridge. Climb slowly up a small valley northwest of Cole Mountain. At the head of this valley, follow the trail as it swings west and northwest to meet **Old Adams Road** near the **Appalachian Trail** (AT) after about 2.2 miles.

From here you have a number of options. You could follow the AT to Saddle Ball Mountain and Mt. Greylock or use the Old Adams Road to return via the Cheshire Harbor Trail, among others.

SILVERFOX TRAIL
Distance: 1.3 miles (approximately)
Estimated time: 1 hour
Blazes: Blue
Map location: M – 7
Maintenance: Department of Conservation and Recreation, Adams Sno-Drifters Snowmobile Club

This trail provides a route from Redgate Road to Old Adams Road.

HOW TO GET THERE
• Refer to directions for the Cheshire Harbor Trail (page 130).

DESCRIPTION
From the **Cheshire Harbor Trail** trailhead, follow the abandoned continuation of West Mountain Road. After about 0.4 mi., the **Redgate Road** leaves to the right (west) just before Bassett Brook. Follow it. The grade is obvious and a single blaze has been chopped in the bark of a sixteen-inch tree.

Soon you will cross a bridge. The Silverfox Trail continues straight ahead while the Redgate Road turns left and crosses a second bridge. This new trail is used mostly by snowmobiles in winter and may be difficult to follow.

From Redgate Road it is about 1.3 mi. to **Old Adams Road**. There you may turn right to reach the Cheshire Harbor Trail or left to the **Appalachian Trail**.

THUNDERBOLT TRAIL

Distance: 1.6 miles to Appalachian Trail
Estimated time: 2.0 hours
Blazes: Blue
Map location: N – 10
Maintenance: Department of Conservation and Recreation, Thunderbolt Ski Club

Skiing as a sport did not gain popularity in the United States until the 1930s. The Mount Greylock Ski Club fueled its growth in the Berkshires and helped lay out the Thunderbolt Ski Trail. In the fall of 1934, 30 Civilian Conservation Corps members cleared this 1.6-mile trail 2,175 vertical feet down the east side of Mt. Greylock.

Skiers competed in sanctioned races on the Thunderbolt trail through the mid-1950s. In 1948 Per Klippgen set the record of two minutes and nine seconds, top-to-bottom: an average speed of about 45 miles per hour! With enough snow cover, it is still possible to ski the Thunderbolt Trail (*Most Excellent Majesty*).

HOW TO GET THERE

- Drive east on Route 2 from Williamstown.
- As you enter North Adams (5.0 mi.) follow signs to Down town, Route 8 south, and Heritage State Park; bear right to Main Street and a stoplight.
- Take Route 8 south (5.1 mi.).
- At the Monument to President McKinley in Adams, turn right (west) onto Maple St. (10.4 mi.).
- Pass a cemetery and turn left after 0.4 mi. on West Road (10.8 mi.).
- After another 0.4 mi. turn right on Gould Road (11.2 mi. total) at a sign for Greylock Glen.
- Follow Gould Road for 0.4 mi. and then continue straight on Thiel Road where Gould Road turns left (11.6 mi.).
- Drive 0.5 mi. to a trailhead, marked with a sign for the Thunderbolt Trail and Bellows Pipe (12.1 mi.). If you cross a minor brook (Hoxie) you have gone too far.

DESCRIPTION

From Thiel Road, follow the right (north) of two trails, a dirt road along the south side of Hoxie Brook. You will pass a turnoff to the left, then arrive at a sharp switchback, also to the left. Where a trail goes right across Hoxie Brook, toward **Ragged Mountain** to the north, turn left.

There is a switchback in the trail right after contouring under a very steep slope. As you climb, you follow the steep valley of Hoxie Brook. At the next intersection, a spur trail to the left takes you to a lookout and berries in late summer. Back on the Thunderbolt Trail, keep climbing along Hoxie Brook to a junction with the **Bellows Pipe Trail**.

To the left, the Bellows Pipe Extension leads down to Gould Farm on a more gentle grade, a better descent route than the lower Thunderbolt Trail. From here, you climb a ridiculously steep grade that includes the famous drops and turns ski racers negotiated: Big Bend, the Needle's Eye, the Big Schuss, and the Schuss. At 1.6 mi. you crest at the **Appalachian Trail** (1.6 mi.). Turn left on the AT to reach the Greylock Summit (2.0 mi.).

GREYLOCK GLEN

To access the trails described in Greylock East, you must pass through Greylock Glen, a 1,000-acre site above the town of Adams that is home to a growing multi-use trail system. The town, in conjunction with the Commonwealth, has planned for the site to be a hub for outdoor recreation and education.

Once fully developed, the Glen will host a variety of activites including cross-country skiing (skate and classic), single-track mountain biking, snowmobiling, hiking, running, and walking, as well as downhill backcountry skiing.

GREYLOCK SOUTH

Rockwell Road and several trails provide convenient access to Mt. Greylock along Saddle Ball Mountain from the south. A visitor center at the Reservation entrance has maps, information, and restrooms.

ROCKWELL ROAD

Distance: 8.5 miles to Greylock summit
Estimated time: 20 minutes driving from Visitors Center
Map location: H – 1 (Beginning off map)
Blazes: None
Maintenance: Department of Conservation and Recreation

Since its construction in 1906-7, Rockwell Road has been the most used auto road to the summit of Mt. Greylock. From the park Visitor Center to Greylock's summit, the road provides access to many trails and park facilities. In winter months Rockwell Road is groomed and used as a cross-country skiing and snowmobile trail.

HOW TO GET THERE

- Take Route 7 south toward Pittsfield from Williamstown.
- After 13.3 mi. and brown signs for the Visitor Center and Bascom Lodge, turn left on North Main Street.
- Bear right onto Quarry Road at 15.1 miles. A sign directs you to "State Reservation."
- Next, bear left on Rockwell Road (15.5 mi.) by the maintenance facility and enter the Mt. Greylock State Reservation.

DESCRIPTION

From Quarry Road (0.0 mi.), Rockwell Road begins its 8.5-mile ascent of Mt. Greylock. At 0.6 mi., you pass the Visitors Center on the right. Inside is a wealth of print information as well as staff from the Department of Conservation and Recreation, available to answer questions. In winter, a gate closes the road to vehicles beyond this point.

From the visitor center parking you may access the short **Brook and Berry Trail** and **Cliff Trail** in all seasons. The **Northrup Trail** and **Woodason Spring Trail** connect the visitor center loops to Rounds' Rock and Jones' Nose.

Rockwell Road meets the Northrup Trail at about 2.0 miles. A gravel pullout on the right (east) at 3.7 mi. is parking for the **Rounds' Rock Trail** and Woodason Spring Trail. Further along you reach the Jones' Nose day parking area (4.4 mi.) with access to the Northrup Trail, Jones' Nose Trail, **CCC Dynamite Trail**, **Appalachian Trail** (AT), Woodason Spring Trail, **Stage Trail**, and **Old Adams Road**.

After a straight, level stretch, **Greylock Road** enters from the left (5.6 mi.). This steep dirt road connects to Route 7. Slightly farther up the mountain, **Sperry Road** (6.3 mi.) bears left from Rockwell Road.

Rockwell Road begins to climb more steeply from Sperry Road toward the summit. The **Overlook Trail** begins where the road makes a hairpin turn (7.2 mi.). The **Hopper Trail** is also accessible at this point. A second switchback (7.3 mi.) coincides with the AT. Just beyond this, Rockwell Road intersects both the AT and the end of the **Cheshire Harbor Trail**.

Notch Road enters from the northwest (left) at a third crossing of the AT (7.8 mi.) from the south. From this junction, Rockwell Road becomes **Summit Road** and circles Mt. Greylock to the summit (8.5 mi.).

VISITOR CENTER LOOPS

Distances: 2.0 miles (loop)
Estimated time: 1 hour
Blazes: Blue
Map location: H – 1
Maintenance: Department of Conservation and Recreation

These leisurely loops include a self-guided nature trail and provide access to the Northrup and Woodason Spring Trails. Several of the routes beginning at the Visitor Center are suitable for cross-country skiing.

HOW TO GET THERE

- Refer to directions for Rockwell Road (page 137).
- Park at the Visitor Center (16.0 mi.).

DESCRIPTION

The trailhead and information board for the **Brook and Berry Trail** and **Bradley Farm Nature Trail** are located at the far (east) side of the visitor center parking lot. Enter the woods onto a clear path. The trail forks immediately, offering alternate routes for summer and winter use. Keeping to the right, you will cross a brook (0.2 mi.) and pass the trailheads for the **Woodason Spring Trail** (0.7 mi.) and the **Northrup Trail** (0.9 mi.), and then intersect **Rockwell Road** (1.0 mile).

Return the same way, or cross the road to the **Cliff Loop** and return south to the Visitor Center (2.0 mi.).

WOODASON SPRING TRAIL

Distance: 2.7 miles
Estimated time: 1.5 hours (Brook and Berry Trail to Rockwell Road)
Blazes: Blue
Map location: I – 2
Maintenance: Department of Conservation and Recreation

This trail complements the Northrup Trail, providing an eastern route between Jones' Nose Trail, Rounds' Rock and the Visitor Center Loops.

HOW TO GET THERE

- Refer to directions for Rockwell Road (page 137).
- Park at the Visitor Center (16.0 mi.).

DESCRIPTION

The Woodason Spring Trail begins 0.7 mi. along the eastern-most route of the **Brook and Berry Trail**. From its start (0.0 mi.), the trail climbs steadily, paralleling **Rockwell Road** to the west.

Over its length, the trail crosses a series of small brooks and stone walls. Watch for a pair of parallel stone walls (1.6 mi), indicating that a farm road once passed through. Much of the forest in this area is sunny and open, dominated by shrubs that took over once it was abandoned from grazing.

Near its end, the trail crosses another brook (2.5 mi.) and begins a short, steep climb up a ledge. Cross over the top of the ledge to the intersection with Rockwell Road (2.7 mi.). From here, a trail extension leads 0.5 mi. to Jones' Nose and crosses an historic road towards Cheshire. Another option is the **Rounds' Rock Trail**, which begins on the opposite side of the road. If on skis, you need not climb the ledge: stay to the left (south) to meet Rockwell Road.

ROUNDS' ROCK TRAIL
Distance: 0.7 miles (loop)
Estimated time: 30 minutes
Blazes: Blue
Map location: I – 5
Maintenance: Department of Conservation and Recreation

In 1915, the Greylock Commission purchased Rounds' Rock (2,580) and "the finest view of the larger portion of the county anywhere to be obtained" (*Most Excellent Majesty*). A short walk from Rockwell Road rewards you with two fantastic cliff views to the south and west.

HOW TO GET THERE
* Refer to directions for Rockwell Road (page 137).
* Drive 3.1 mi. past the visitor center to a gravel pullout on the right before the Jones' Nose parking.

DESCRIPTION
Carefully cross **Rockwell Road** (0.0 mi.) and enter the forest. A man named Jabez Rounds grazed sheep and tended orchards here in the 1790s. Low bush blueberries peak in August for your picking pleasure.

At the outer end of the loop two spur trails lead to vistas of the Catskills, Connecticut, and Mt. Everett on a clear day. A memorial marks the site of a 1945 plane crash. Follow the loop or retrace your steps to Rockwell Road (0.7 mi.).

NORTHRUP TRAIL
Distance: 3.6 miles
Estimated time: 2 hours
Blazes: Blue
Map location: I – 6
Maintenance: Department of Conservation and Recreation

This level trail shares parking with the Jones' Nose Trail and Old Adams Road. It provides easy access to the short trails and views of Rounds' Rock to the south. In winter it provides a route for skiers to avoid snowmobiles on Rockwell Road.

HOW TO GET THERE
- Refer to directions for Rockwell Road (page 137).
- Drive past the visitor center, into the park, past Rounds' Rock to the Jones' Nose Trailhead (19.9 mi.).

DESCRIPTION
From the parking area (0.0 mi.) cross **Rockwell Road** and enter the woods to the west. Keep to the left as you pass the **Stage Trail**. The Northrup trail contours along the western slope of Rounds' Rock, heading south. After about three-quarters of a mile a short spur connects to the **Rounds' Rock Trail**.

The Northrup Trail continues south to meet up again with Rockwell Road (3.0 mi.). Cross the road and continue to the south. The trail ends at an intersection with the **Brook and Berry Trail** (3.6). From here, it is 0.2 mi. southeast to the **Woodason Spring Trail**, an alternate route back to Rounds' Rock and Jones' Nose parking lot, and 0.9 mi. to the Visitor Center.

STAGE TRAIL
Distance: 0.8 miles
Estimated time: 30 minutes
Blazes: Blue
Map location: I – 6
Maintenance: Department of Conservation and Recreation

This trail shares parking with the Jones' Nose Trail and Old Adams

Road. It follows the route that stage coaches took after climbing old Adams Road. In winter, it provides a route for skiers to avoid snowmobiles on sections of Rockwell and Greylock Roads.

HOW TO GET THERE
- Refer to directions for Rockwell Road (page 137).
- Drive past the visitor center and into the park, past Rounds' Rock to the Jones' Nose Trailhead (19.9 mi.).

DESCRIPTION
From the parking area (0.0 mi.) cross **Rockwell Road** and enter the woods to the west. Keep to the right (north) as you pass the **Northrup Trail**. The Stage Trail follows an old road grade to the north. At 0.7 mi. the trail curves to the left (west) and descends to connect with **Greylock Road**.

JONES' NOSE TRAIL
Distances: 0.5 mile to CCC Dynamite Trail, 1.0 mile to AT
Estimated time: 25 minutes to CCC Dynamite Trail
Blazes: Blue
Map location: I – 6
Maintenance: Department of Conservation and Recreation

Named for a farmer centuries ago, Jones' Nose offers fine views south and west into Connecticut and New York beyond Berkshire County. A short trail climbs through a clearing and then connects to the CCC Dynamite Trail and Appalachian Trail.

HOW TO GET THERE
- Refer to directions for Rockwell Road (page 137).
- Drive past the visitor center and into the park, past Rounds' Rock to the Jones' Nose Trailhead and parking lot (19.9 mi.).

DESCRIPTION
From the parking area (0.0 mi.), hike north up the slope of Jones' Nose. After a quarter mile of views you enter the forest and continue to climb gradually towards Saddle Ball Mountain. At 0.5 mi., the **CCC Dynamite Trail** branches off to the left

(north). There are good views west to the **Taconic Range** at 0.7 miles. You reach the **Appalachian Trail** at 1.0 mi. on the ridge of Saddle Ball Mountain.

CCC DYNAMITE TRAIL

Distance: 1.5 miles
Estimated time: 50 minutes
Blazes: Blue
Map location: I – 7
Maintenance: Department of Conservation and Recreation

This trail was built in 1990 and named for the explosives the Civilian Conservation Corps (CCC) stored in the area for construction of roads and trails in the 1930s. In spring and early summer this relatively flat trail is a favorite for viewing ferns and wildflowers.

HOW TO GET THERE:
- Refer to the Jones' Nose Trail description; the CCC Dynamite Trail starts on top of Jones' Nose.

DESCRIPTION
From the **Jones' Nose Trail** (0.0 mi.), bear left (north) at the signed junction for the CCC Dynamite Trail. You will hike nearly due-north on a course along the western flank of Saddle Ball Mountain. If you look carefully, you may see the remains of crates used to store explosives decades ago.

At 1.5 mi., you reach **Rockwell Road**. **Sperry Road** continues north to a campground and a number of trails, including the **Hopper Trail** to the summit of Mt. Greylock.

GREYLOCK ROAD
Distance: 3.5 miles (approximately)
Estimated time: 10 minutes driving
Blazes: None
Map location: F – 8
Maintenance: Town of New Ashford, Department of Conservation and Recreation

Many roads used to climb the slopes of Greylock from all sides, including this one. Today, Notch and Rockwell Roads are the primary routes into the Reservation and to the summit. Greylock Road used to provide secondary access from Route 7, but is no longer accessible by automobile. This steep dirt road does serve as a fine, stout bike route.

HOW TO GET THERE
* Take Route 7 south toward Pittsfield from Williamstown.
* At 8.7 mi. turn left (east) beyond Roys Road at either of two entrances.

DESCRIPTION
After a ninety-degree left turn, Greylock Road heads east on a steady grade and crosses the headwaters of East Branch of the Green River near the junction with old Bauers Road. Soon after, a gate marks the Mt. Greylock State Reservation Boundary. A northward, contouring climb brings you to **Rockwell Road** about 3.5 mi. from Route 7.

APPALACHIAN TRAIL
MT. GREYLOCK FROM CHESHIRE
Distance: 6.8 miles to Greylock Summit
Estimated time: 4.5 hours
Map location: L – 4
Blazes: White
Maintenance: AMC Mass. AT Committee

Although many use the Appalachian Trail (AT) for long-distance backpacking, it also provides excellent day hiking opportunities in the area. This section of the AT is the principal southern access to the Greylock Range. Along the way are a number of historic coach roads as well as the upgraded automobile roads of today.

HOW TO GET THERE
- From the junction of Routes 2 and 7, take Route 2 east to the junction with Route 8 in North Adams (5.1 mi.).
- Go south on Route 8 to stoplight in Cheshire (15.7 mi.).
- Turn left (east) on Church St. and proceed to the Ashuwillticook Trail parking lot (just past the Post Office).
- The AT (northbound) travels west on Church St.

DESCRIPTION
From the Ashuwillticook Trail parking area, proceed west on Church Street. Turn right onto School Street at a trail kiosk and replica of a cheese press with an historic plaque. Continue on School Street before turning sharply left into a small field just past the Cheshire Community/Senior Center. Walk through a short stretch of woods and around a gate into an agricultural field. Proceed through the field, cross Route 8, walk around another gate, and climb to another agricultural field.

The AT turns sharply left into the woods and continues a moderate climb until reaching another open field with eastward-facing views. Reynolds Rock, a large outcrop, appears on the left (and may be climbed for yet another easterly view) just before reaching Outlook Avenue (1.4 mi.).

After crossing Outlook Avenue, the AT descends briefly into a slightly wet area between two more fields and continues west along the edge before turning to enter the woods at the open area's far end. The trail continues through a small stream and wet area, crosses a power line (1.6), and then begins a steady ascent, crossing minor intermittent streams. The trail crosses into the drainage of Kitchen Brook and climbs steeply through hemlocks as the land drops sharply to the left.

A sharp right turn brings you out of the drainage, and the trail ascends a series of short cliffs between relatively flat areas, eventually crossing **Old Adams Road** (4.1 mi.). As you continue northbound on the AT, the trail climbs steeply on rock steps and reaches a small viewpoint to the south before climbing again. The blue-blazed side trail to Mark Noepel Shelter (sleeps 10) and the Bassett Brook campsite (privy, two tent platforms, four tent sites) is reached at 5.0 mi.

Climb past this side trail and reach the upper (north) end of **Jones' Nose Trail** (5.6 mi.). The AT turns sharply right to continue along the ridge of Saddle Ball Mountain through a stunted balsam forest which provides habitat for the rare Bicknell's Thrush and several rare plants. At the end of the ridge, the trail descends to cross a sphagnum swamp on extensive bog bridging and meets **Rockwell Road** and a day-use parking area (6.7 mi.).

The northbound AT does not cross the road, but continues over a small hill for 0.3 mi. before descending again to cross Rockwell Road at the intersection of the **Cheshire Harbor Trail**. Crossing the road leads to the the intersection with the **Hopper Trail**.

Continue past the Hopper Trail as the AT skirts the edge of a former water-supply pond and its pump house; then, at 7.2 mi., cross the three-way junction of Rockwell Road, **Notch Road** and **Summit Road** before heading into the woods for the final steep climb to the summit.

As you exit the woods, the trail enters a parking area for summit workers (no public parking) near a large radio tower. Composting toilets are available here. Continue across Summit Road and very briefly through a group of stunted trees, and the AT emerges into the summit's open area. **Bascom Lodge** (open mid-May to mid-October) is visible on the right. The AT continues straight ahead, past a bronze model of the Greylock mountain range, before climbing steps to the base of the War Memorial tower (7.7 mi.). The tower is open to the public, and an internal stairway climbs to an enclosed viewing area.

Pine branch drawing by Katie Craig '08

HIKING IN THE NORTHEAST

The North Berkshire area is wonderfully accessible and filled with endless fields, peaks, and valleys worth exploring. However, there are other areas farther away that can also be explored with the help of transportation.

Nearby, Central and South Berkshire County have numerous pleasant walks and hikes. Refer to *Hikes and Walks in Berkshire County* or *A Guide to Natural Places in Berkshire County* for more information. To explore other parts of Massachusetts, including the Hoosac Range and Route 2 corridor directly east of Williamstown, check out the *AMC Massachusetts and Rhode Island Trail Guide*.

North along Route 7, the Green Mountains of Vermont stretch over 200 miles to Canada. The *Long Trail Guide* and *Day Hikes in Vermont* published by the Green Mountain Club describe the hundreds of trails available.

Only three hours away, the Adirondack Mountains of upstate New York draw visitors to the mountains and rivers of the six-million-acre Adirondack State Park. The Adirondack Mountain Club publishes a series of guides, each one devoted to a region of the park.

Farther east, the highest peaks of New England are found in the White Mountains of New Hampshire. Alpine terrain, glacial valleys, waterfalls, the Appalachian Mountain Club (AMC) huts, and an extensive trail network attract hikers to the area. The AMC publishes the *White Mountain Guide*, now in its 28th edition.

Stretching from Georgia to Maine, the Appalachian Trail passes through southern New York, Connecticut, Massachusetts, Vermont, and New Hampshire. The Appalachian Trail Conservancy publishes a guide series if you wish to follow part or all of this famous path.

Mt. Katahdin in Maine's Baxter State Park is a mecca for many New England hikers as the northern terminus of the Appalachian Trail. Another attraction in Maine is Cadillac Mountain in Acadia National Park; on some days of the year, it is the first point in the continental United States that sunlight hits directly.

Refer to the bibliography for more complete information on the references mentioned above.

WINTER

> With the falling of the leaves, the masks of green are stripped off the hillsides, revealing the diversity and uniqueness of each ridge and valley, rock and stream, old shed or oil well hitherto unseen. It is in the winter, when the hills bare their innermost selves, that we get to know them. Then, in the spring...we can look at the hills as old friends few others understand.
>
> - John W. Walker

Winter weather: some find it intimidating, others find it challenging. Some consider it just plain fun. Whether you're planning a short snowshoe tour through the woods on a chilly morning, a midnight adventure up Pine Cobble in the storm of the century, or a backpacking trip on a rainy summer day, cold weather presents its own threats and rewards.

This section outlines some things to keep in mind when planning a trip that might include cold weather. Although these tips are generalized as winter safety, be aware that wind and rain on the summit of Mt. Greylock can make an August day more dangerous than a clear, cold day in February. With preparation and common sense, however, both can be safe and fun.

SHORTER DAYS

We all know that winter means shorter days, but we don't always take that into consideration when planning trips. Be sure to carry headlamps, get an early start, and remember that the pace at which you travel may be significantly slower than it is at other times of year. While three miles per hour might be realistic during the summer, snow and ice may reduce your pace to less than one mile per hour during winter. When the snow is deep and finding a route becomes a challenge, covering one mile may take even more time.

DEHYDRATION

Hypothermia and frostbite are two of the most obvious cold-related problems you might encounter during winter, but they aren't the only ones. Dehydration, which "thickens" your blood and decreases its rate of flow, can cause headaches, exhaustion, and an increased susceptibility to frostbite. Cold, dry winter air removes more moisture from each of your breaths, and the cold temperatures decrease your thirst response as well.

Drink all the time, whether or not you are thirsty. You should drink at least two quarts on a day hike, and 5-6 quarts a day if you are winter camping. For extended camping trips, pack herbal teas instead of coffee or hot cocoa (the caffeine in these drinks can exacerbate dehydration).

NUTRITION

Exposure to cold air constantly drains heat away from your body, so you need a large number of calories simply to stay warm. While most people probably won't need to eat sticks of butter, as some mountaineers do, you will need to allow even more food than you would for normal outdoor activity (up to 4,000-6,000 calories per person per day).

Adding to this challenge, cold temperatures make consuming your food more difficult. For example, you might have to break your candy bar into bite-size pieces with a pocket knife if it freezes solid! In preparation, put your trail snacks in an inner jacket pocket to keep them warm. Also, fill your water bottle with hot water and stick it in a pair of socks for insulation. Ice forms at the top of water, so store the bottle upside-down…just make sure it doesn't leak.

COLD

An obvious challenge of winter recreation is the ever-present cold. The antidote is heat, which we need to generate and retain through movement and insulation. Stay active in the cold, and as long as you eat and drink enough (see above) your body can generate plenty of heat. With proper clothing (see What to Wear) you can capture that precious heat and stay dry along the way.

Cold Weather Tips

- Wear a hat.

- Wear a sock/boot combination with room to wiggle your toes.

- Bundle up your torso and legs to keep your extremities warm, and swing your arms/legs to force blood to your hands and feet.

- Be sure to wear a shell in the wind: this will keep your heat from being swept away.

- During rest breaks: walk around or jump up-and-down to generate heat.

- If camping: heat up water to put in a Nalgene or metal bottle, wrap the bottle in a sock, and place in sleeping bag for a warm sleep. You can also exercise lightly before getting into your sleeping bag to pre-heat your body.

ICE AND SNOW

Even if snow at the base of a mountain is well packed or shallow, don't rely on either of these being true as you gain altitude. A few feet of powder can become a tiring obstacle, so carry skis or snowshoes if you are likely to be traveling on unbroken trails. If you intend to hike above treeline or try some technical climbing in winter, evaluate your skill level carefully. Go with more experienced people or hire a guide if necessary.

As is true for all activities, there are dangers associated with winter sports. The majority of these, however, are simply due to poor preparation and bad decisions. If you travel in groups and stay dry, fed, and well-hydrated, winter activities can provide some of your most wonderful moments outdoors. Despite all of the potential problems, breaking trail through fresh powder, climbing a frozen waterfall, or battling against high winds on an icy ridge can be both exhilarating and rewarding.

WINTER ACTIVITIES

Snow and ice provide an opportunity for different modes of travel in the North Berkshire Hills. Unfortunately, the vagaries of weather may deny you snow when you most want it, but usually winter allows at least a couple of months with snowcover — more at higher elevations. When the snow is shallow or firm, hiking is the best way to go on local trails. But when deeper snow slows you down, snowshoeing and skiing are fun ways to explore. Snow-making keeps the downhill ski areas running from Christmas into spring. For those who like ice, crampons and ice axes can take you on icy mountain ridges or up frozen waterfalls.

SNOWSHOEING

The advent of modern aluminum and plastic snowshoes has fueled an explosion of snowshoeing across the country. The snowshoe is a simple concept: its large surface area keeps you from sinking and reduces the fatigue of "postholing" with each step. You do not need special boots. Any warm, comfortable ones will do. All trails in this guide may be snowshoed, especially the steeper or more narrow trails that may be difficult to ski. With some basic navigation skills, you can explore freely off the trails since snow minimizes your impact. The Williams Outing Club (WOC) Equipment Room has many pairs of snowshoes for use by members.

CROSS-COUNTRY SKIING

Rather than the adrenaline rush of zooming down a mountain on downhill skis, cross-country (Nordic) skiing offers the peaceful serenity of snow-covered woods. It is one of the best forms of cardiovascular exercise because it involves all major muscle groups and is easier on the joints than running or even walking.

Cross-country skiing in this guide refers to groomed terrain or lower-elevation, valley routes close to population centers. The more challenging and remote terrain of the mountains above is classified as Backcountry Skiing and is described separately.

Nordic skiing is also one of the most environmentally friendly outdoor sports because snow cushions the trails from any significant impact. Safety is less of an issue than with downhill skiing, but you should listen for snowmobiles that could be in the area. Falling is not uncommon and can be fun, especially if you use the classic sit-down-crash method. Sometimes steep hills are tricky, but as long as you control your speed and keep your poles pointed behind you (so that they don't stab you when crashing), the impact is usually cushioned by snow.

WOC members may use the Nordic ski equipment available in the Equipment Room. During Winter Study, WOC offers cross-country classes and transportation to local trails. For more information, refer to Lauren Stevens' *Skiing in the Berkshire Hills*.

Taconic Golf Course

The golf course is located on the south side of Weston Field, on the edge of the Williams College campus. Gentle slopes and open terrain make this a great area for the first-time skier.

Stone Hill

A beautiful place to ski, although there are some steeper sections above The Clark. Zigzag up a steep hill so your skis can grip on a more gradual angle. Refer to the trail descriptions or simply explore the pastures.

Hopkins Forest

Hopkins Forest is a good place to try some steeper terrain, especially on the upper loop. Use the trail description in this guide.

Field Farm

This flat land managed by The Trustees of Reservations has 4.5 miles of trail along forest, field, marsh, and pond. Refer to the description in the Taconic Range section of this guide.

Greylock Glen

A network of trails used extensively by snowmobiles above the town of Adams. There are some skier-only trails.

CROSS-COUNTRY SKI AREAS

Always call ahead to check if the following areas have enough snow to open. You can also look for other Berkshire cross-country skiing areas at xcskimass.com.

Mount Greylock Ski Club, Williamstown, MA.
A small downhill and cross-country area in Goodell Hollow along Roaring Brook on the west side of Mt. Greylock.
mtgreylockskiclub.com
(413) 445-7887

Notch View, Windsor, MA.
Trustees of Reservations land with groomed cross-country ski trails.
thetrustees.org
(413) 684-0148

Prospect Mountain, Woodford, Vermont.
With a base at 2,250 feet, Prospect has the most reliable skiing in the area.
prospectmountain.com
(802) 442-2575

Stump Sprouts, Hawley, MA.
Cross-country and backcountry skiing. A high elevation usually promises good snow.
stumpsprouts.com
(413) 339-4265

BACKCOUNTRY SKIING

The Williamstown area offers almost unlimited opportunities for backcountry skiing expeditions. Once you've learned basic cross-country skiing techniques, cold weather travel and navigation, you are ready to journey into the hills. Blazed trails are a logical place to start, but feel free to explore throughout the hills as your skills and knowledge increase. Reread the Starting Out section and Winter Sports introduction for a few preparation and safety reminders.

The ski equipment you use on flat or groomed trails can be

used on more challenging terrain, but eventually you will want to investigate heavier equipment, telemark skiing, and alpine touring (AT). Telemark skiing and alpine touring use stiffer boots, wider skis with metal edges, and sturdy free-heel binding systems to negotiate backcountry terrain.

Below is a list of local trails well-suited to skiing, with a few notes for each. Other trails are steep or narrow and must be ascended by switchbacking through the forest or on telemark or AT skis with skins for uphill traction. Refer to the hiking trail descriptions for specific directions.

GREEN MOUNTAINS
Dome Trail
Watch for snowmobiles. The top part may be difficult to follow.

TACONIC RANGE
Hopkins Forest
See Cross-Country Skiing, above.
Birch Brook Trail
Good loop with R.R.R. Brooks trail.
Fitch Trail
Somewhat steep, up Bee Hill; advanced.
R.R.R. Brooks Trail
Beautiful gradual climb to the Taconic Crest. Lower section may be treacherous with little or icy snow.
Sara Tenney Trail
Old roads and alternate routes designed for skiing; an alternative route to the R.R.R. Brooks Trail.
Shepherd's Well Trail
Completes R.R.R. Brooks Trail to Taconic Crest Trail (TCT); combine with Birch Brook Trail and TCT.
WRLF Loop Trail
A flat logging grade makes for a short, gentle ski.
Berlin Pass Trail
Sustained climb, good access for downhill runs at the Old Williams College Ski Area.
Old Williams College Ski Area
A fun, steep descent from Berlin Mountain for advanced skiers.

Field Farm
See Cross-Country Skiing, above.

Taconic Crest Trail
High and often windy.

Old Petersburg Ski Area
Abandoned and partially overgrown downhill ski trails south of Petersburg Pass.

GREYLOCK RANGE

Money Brook Trail
After second bridge, take cut-off south to the Hopper Trail to return to the trailhead.

Roaring Brook Trail
Consistently demanding climb; advanced. Descend Stony Ledge Trail.

Stony Ledge Trail
Originally cut as a downhill trail; advanced (see below).

Notch Road
Steep road with snowmobile traffic.

Bellows Pipe Trail
To summit of Greylock; steepest at top.

Old Summit Road
Bypasses Notch Road near Mt. Williams.

Cheshire Harbor Trail
Popular route up Greylock with snowmobile traffic.

Old Adams Road
Snowmobiles.

Thunderbolt Trail
THE ski descent of the area. For experienced back-country or downhill skiers (see below).

Redgate Road
Snowmobiles.

Silverfox Trail
Snowmobiles.

Rockwell Road
Heavy snowmobile traffic.

Brook and Berry Trails
Short loops near Mount Greylock Visitor Center.

Northrup Trail
Alternative to Rockwell Road.
CCC Dynamite Trail
Alternative to Rockwell Road.
Sperry Road
Part of the Roaring Brook – Stony Ledge loop.

Note: When skiing anywhere in the Mt. Greylock Reservation, be aware that the Department of Conservation and Recreation may occasionally change the trail uses (i.e. snowmobiles only or skiing only). It is your responsibility to find out what the current usage regulations are, and to obey them.

BACKCOUNTRY SKI DESCENTS

A few trails in the area were cut specifically for downhill skiing between the 1930s–1950s. These are challenging runs for advanced backcountry or downhill skiers.

THUNDERBOLT SKI TRAIL
Distance: 1.6 miles
Vertical drop: 2,175 feet
Map location: N – 10

This exceptionally fast, difficult trail descends the east slope of Mt. Greylock from the summit to Thiel Farm, west of Adams. The breathtaking descent earned its name from a rollercoaster at Revere Beach, an amusement park outside Boston. In 1938, it was the site of the Eastern Downhill Championships, which attracted a crowd of 6,000 people. Under favorable conditions, such as deep powder or heavy spring snow, it can be an exciting experience for the advanced skier. Refer to the hiking trail description.

STONY LEDGE SKI TRAIL
Distance: 2.1 miles
Vertical drop: 1,400 feet
Map location: H – 10

Like the Thunderbolt, the Civilian Conservation Corps constructed this trail with the Mt. Greylock Ski Club for downhill skiers. The trail hasn't been maintained for skiing; brush may be a problem except with a couple feet of snow. This steep, challenging trail descends from Stony Ledge at the end of Sperry Road to Goodell Hollow in Williamstown. For a loop, ascend the more gradual, though still challenging, Roaring Brook Trail. Refer to the hiking trail description.

DOWNHILL SKI AREAS
If you want to improve your skiing skills or avoid the uphill climbing inherent in free-heel skiing, head to one of the many downhill ski areas within an hour of Williamstown.

NORTH BERKSHIRE COUNTY
Jiminy Peak, Hancock
www.jiminypeak.com
(413) 738-5500

Mount Greylock Ski Club, Williamstown
www.mtgreylockskiclub.com
(413) 445-7887

OTHER MASSACHUSETTS
Berkshire East, Charlemont
www.berkshireeast.com
(413) 339-6618

Bousquet, Pittsfield
www.bosquets.com
(413) 442-8316

Butternut, Great Barrington
www.skibutternut.com
(413) 528-2000

Catamount, South Egremont
www.catamountski.com
(413) 528-1262

Otis Ridge, Otis
www.otisridge.com
(413) 269-4444

SOUTHERN VERMONT
Bromley, Manchester Center
www.bromley.com
(802) 824-5522

Mount Snow, West Dover
www.mountsnow.com
(802) 464-3333

Stratton Mountain, Stratton
www.stratton.com
(802) 297-4000

ICE CLIMBING

Modern waterfall ice climbing evolved from mountaineering in the
20th century. New England winters produce significant amounts of
ice on mountain crags from the Berkshires to Canada.

The sport relies on specialized equipment including stiff boots,
crampons, ice axes, helmets, a climbing rope, and anchor hardware.
You also need specific knowledge to safely climb ice.

If ice climbing interests you, contact the Williams Outing Club or
a guide service to get an introduction to this sport.

BIKING

A bike ride provides an excellent opportunity for adventure and exploration in the Williamstown area, bringing you closer to some of the gorgeous scenery in the region. Whether on trails or local roads, the riding in and around town is superb, and the possibilities range from easy excursions for beginners to more extreme rides for the experienced cyclist.

To ensure fun, successful rides, all cyclists should follow a few basic safety guidelines. Wear a helmet to protect your head, and glasses to shield your eyes from sand, mud, and sticks. Gloves are not absolutely necessary, but they will protect your hands if you crash. Perhaps the best way to prevent a serious problem when riding is to stay within your ability and comfort level, as accidents usually happen when you get tired and begin to make mistakes. On that note, consider riding with another person so that someone is around to help if you do have an accident or get lost.

No matter what kind of bike you have, be sure to keep it in good condition. Clean it on a regular basis, and take it to a local bike shop for periodic tune-ups. Before each ride, check to see that the brakes are working, and that the seat height is properly adjusted (your knee should be slightly bent when at the bottom of the pedal stroke). Always carry a patch kit, a pump, water (drink one bottle per hour). If you are going out for more than an hour, you should also consider bringing some food, warm clothes, and extra tools.

MOUNTAIN BIKING

Mountain biking has become an increasingly popular activity in the Williamstown area. It allows access to gorgeous scenery without the traffic that can be a problem for bikers on the road. Possibilities for exploration include miles of old logging roads and some hiking trails.

Because of the increasing number of people mountain biking, it is important that riders do their best to minimize impact on the trails. This means not riding when trails are extremely wet (especially in the spring) and not skidding by locking up your brakes. Respect posted signs indicating trail restrictions and do not ride on trails marked "Hiking only." Always respect the rights of private land owners, and ask for permission before riding on their land.

While you are on the trail, it is important to respect other trail users including hikers and individuals on horseback or all-terrain vehicle (ATV). Slow down or dismount when approaching hikers or horseback riders, and let them know when you are behind them. When you see or hear an ATV approaching, be sure to move out of the way. Remember that our relationship with other trail users determines future access to our favorite trails!

If you are new to mountain biking, try riding some local roads first and then move on to trails. Stop by Williamstown's local bike shop, The Spoke, to get an introduction to the area. A lot of rides around here gain significant elevation, so be ready. Thankfully, what goes up must come down!

DIRT ROADS

Many roads change from pavement to dirt as you get farther away from commercial and more populated areas. These dirt roads often access double-track roads or single-track trails. Refer to the map and location grid to find these roads, and link them together to form longer rides.

Northwest Hill Road
Map location: G – 20
This well-maintained dirt road passes open fields, a great look at the Taconic and Greylock Ranges and some classic wooded areas. Follow directions to **Hopkins Forest Loop Trail** and ride past the entrance of Hopkins Forest.

Bee Hill Road
Map location: G – 18
A steep climb from Route 7 to the south of town with amazing views of Stone Hill, the Hopper and Greylock. An abandoned extension across Route 2 links up with Berlin Mountain Road. To get there, ride south on Routes 2 and 7 from Field Park. Bee Hill Road is the second road to the right after crossing Hemlock Brook.

Berlin Mountain Road
Map location: E – 17
Part of the original Boston - Albany post road and access to the **Old Williams College Ski Area** and **Berlin Pass Trail**. Refer to directions for the Berlin Pass Trail or access it from Bee Hill Road and the abandoned Bee Hill Road extension across Route 2.

White Oaks Road
Map location: I – 21
This road turns to dirt in Vermont near the **Broad Brook** and **Dome Trails**. As the labyrinth of eroded road grades in the area are on private land, please respect postings and land-owners. Stay on Benedict Road and cross the town-owned Rattlesnake watershed to access Mason Hill Road.

Mason Hill Road
Map location: H – 22
From Route 7 in Pownal, Vermont, Mason Hill Road climbs steeply above the Hoosic River Valley to a fantastic view of the Taconic Range.

County Road
   Map location: K – 27
   A several hour, challenging ride from Pownal Center to Stamford, Vermont. Not dry and rideable until late spring. Make sure you are in good shape and leave enough time before dark.

TRAILS

Many trails in the North Berkshire area are open to Mountain Biking, others are definitely closed, and some are specifically posted. Please respect official trail restrictions to protect bike access in the future and when status is uncertain try to contact a landowner or public land agency before you ride.

   For directions, refer to the hiking trail descriptions by using the index. Remember that the estimated times in the descriptions are for hiking, not biking. Below is a list of trails definitely open to mountain bikes, consider all others described in this guide closed unless you see a posting specifically open to bikes.

STONE HILL
   Pasture Trail
      Closed in woods, pasture open.
   Stone Hill Road Trail
      Open, make part of a loop.

GREEN MOUNTAINS
   Dome Trail
      Open, lower half.

TACONIC RANGE
   Berlin Pass Trail
      Open, gullied and rocky.
   Old Williams College Ski Area
      Open, but steep.
   Phelps Trail
      Open, steep in places.

Mills Hollow Trail
Open, road grade to Crest.

**Note: Bikes are strictly prohibited on all trails in Hopkins
Forest due to ongoing research.**

GREYLOCK RANGE
Greylock Road
Open, dirt road up Greylock.
Notch Road
Open, steep paved road.
Cheshire Harbor Trail
Open, popular route.
Old Adams Road
Open, access from Cheshire Harbor Trail to Rockwell Road.
Silverfox Trail
Open, east side up to Old Adams Road.
Greylock Glen
Open in some areas.
Rockwell Road
Open, gradual paved road.
Sperry Road
Open, road to Stony Ledge.

BENNINGTON, VT
BATS (Bennington Area Trail System)
BATS is the most mountain bike-friendly trail system
near Williamstown. There are miles of trails that are well-
marked and maintained. Visit www.batsvt.org for more
information.

ROAD BIKING

There are a number of easily accessible and beautiful loops in the Williamstown area, ranging in length from 10 miles to more than 70. Some are virtually flat, while others include one or more steep and challenging climbs. A small selection of possible rides is described below. Refer to *Bike Rides in the Berkshire Hills* for more routes. You can always use the *North Berkshire Trails* map to plan your own loops. For areas farther away consult maps available from the Williams Outing Club or the Spoke.

When you ride on the road, do not forget that you are a vehicle. You need to make yourself as visible as you can to cars that may not be able to see you very well. Wear bright colors, and make sure that your bike is equipped with lights and reflectors. Obey all traffic rules and regulations, and know the appropriate hand signals to make when you are turning or stopping.

The routes are listed in order of length from shortest to longest.

ASHUWILLTICOOK RAIL TRAIL
Distance: Your choice
Estimated time: Your choice
Elevation change: Minimal

Universally accessible, this paved path offers traffic-free recreation along the Hoosic River from Lanesboro to Adams.

DESCRIPTION
The Ashuwillticook Rail Trail begins at the southeastern entrance of the Berkshire Mall in Lanesboro and follows a historic rail corridor 11.2 mi. to the Discover the Berkshires Visitor Center on Depot Street in the center of Adams, with access points and parking along the way. Contact the Department of Conservation and Recreation for more information.

The trail is open to all sorts of non-motorized recreation, so cyclists may find themselves dodging strollers, roller-skaters, and families. It is a good choice for a casual ride, though, and offers views of the Cheshire Reservoir and Hoosic River.

FIVE CORNERS

Distance: 9.8 miles
Estimated time: 45 minutes to 1 hour
Elevation change: Minimal

Very popular with runners as well as with cyclists, the combination of gentle terrain and relatively short distance make this a pleasant introductory ride. There is one moderate uphill directly north of Five Corners, but after that it is downhill until Williamstown!

DESCRIPTION

Ride east on Route 2, past the Williamstown Savings Bank. Turn right onto Water Street (Route 43) and follow it to "Five Corners," the intersection of Routes 7 and 43 in South Williamstown (5.0 mi.). Turn right onto Route 7 and return to Williamstown. Or turn around and return the way you came for a gradual downhill.

NORTHWEST HILL ROAD

Distance: 11.3 miles
Estimated time: 1 hour
Elevation gain: Minimal

This relatively well-maintained dirt road offers lots of open fields, a great look at the Taconic Mountains, and some classic wooded areas.

DESCRIPTION

From Field Park, take Route 7 north to Bulkley Street (0.4 mi.). Turn left on Bulkley Street; continue across the bridge and up the hill to the T-intersection with Northwest Hill Road (1.2 mi.). Turn right onto Northwest Hill Road, and follow it until you reach Route 346 (6.1 mi.). Take a right on Route 346 and follow it south to Route 7 and continue to Williamstown.

LUCE ROAD – RESERVOIR ROAD
Distance: 12.7 miles
Estimated time: 1.5 hours
Elevation Change: 700 feet

Although the road near the reservoir tends to be a bit rough, this route provides a good alternative to Route 2 when your destination is somewhere south of North Adams. Near the reservoir there is a very good view of the Purple Valley, along with a close-up look at Mt. Prospect and Mt. Williams.

DESCRIPTION
Ride east on Route 2 to Luce Road and turn right (1.5 mi.). Ride uphill a couple miles toward Mt. Prospect, past the reservoirs (The road changes from Luce to Pattison as you cross the town line), and bear right onto Notch Road. Follow Notch Road to a junction with Reservoir Road (5.3 mi.). From here, turn left (downhill) onto Reservoir Road and continue to North Adams and the intersection with Route 8 (7.9 mi.). Go left onto Route 8, and turn left again to follow Route 2 west back to Williamstown.

POWNAL CENTER LOOP
Distance: 16.8 miles
Estimated time: 1 to 2 hours
Elevation change: about 400 feet

One of the nicest short loops around, this ride has fine views and some moderate hills. The road from Pownal Center to North Pownal is second only to Greylock in downhill fun and excitement.

DESCRIPTION
From Field Park, follow Route 7 north out of Williamstown. Continue along Route 7 up the hill that begins at the Green Mountain Park. At Pownal Center (7.8 mi.), take a left on North Pownal Road and coast downhill. In North Pownal, turn left onto Route 346 (9.7 mi.). Route 346 leads back to Route 7 (11.8 mi.), turn right (downhill) to return to Williamstown.

RIVER ROAD – MIDDLE/CROSS ROADS

Distance: 17.0 miles Cross Road, 20.2 miles Middle Road
Estimated time: 2 hours
Elevation Change: 400 feet

This route provides a useful alternative to Route 2 when your destination is somewhere north of North Adams. Middle and Cross Roads are also worth riding in their own right. Both are enjoyable, quiet rides on a plateau to the north of North Adams. The ascent to the plateau is a shockingly steep, but mercifully short, hill.

DESCRIPTION

Ride east on Route 2 and take a left on Cole Avenue. At the end of Cole Avenue, turn right onto North Hoosac Road and follow it to North Adams, where it emerges one block north of Route 2. Follow Route 2 for a short distance until Route 8 branches to the left (6.9 mi.). Take either of the two lefts within the next few miles. The first is Cross Road (8.4 mi.), and the second is Middle Road (10.2 mi.). Both lead back to North Adams at River Street.

ROUTE 43 – BRODIE MOUNTAIN ROAD

Distance: 28.8 miles
Riding Time: 2 to 3 hours
Elevation Change: 900 feet

The enjoyable rolling terrain along Route 43 could well have been designed specifically for biking. Brodie Mountain Road is a good early-season introduction to a moderate hill climb. Beware of the heavy traffic on the final leg of this loop.

DESCRIPTION

Ride east on Route 2 to the intersection of Routes 2 and 43 (Water Street) and turn right. Stay on Route 43 through the intersection with Route 7 and turn left on Brodie Mountain Road, marked "Jiminy Peak Ski Area" (13.8 mi.). This road climbs a moderate hill and ends on a sharp downhill corner at Route 7 (16.4 mi.). Be careful. Return to Williamstown via Route 7 or in combination with Route 43.

PETERSBURG PASS
Distance: 28.8 miles
Estimated time: 2 to 3 hours
Elevation change: 1,400 feet

Although Petersburg Pass is not incredibly steep, and in fact gets easier after the first half mile, it is the longest climb in any of these rides besides Mt. Greylock. The connection with Route 346 makes for an enjoyable and, after the Pass, a very relaxing ride.

DESCRIPTION
Take Routes 2 and 7 south until Route 2 branches right (2.8 mi.). Follow Route 2 up and over Petersburg Pass to its intersection with Route 22. Take Route 22 north to Route 346 (16.2 mi.), then turn right on Route 346 and return to Route 7 (23.8 mi.).

BENNINGTON – ROUTE 22 – ROUTE 346
Distance: 42.6 miles
Estimated time: 3 to 4 hours
Elevation change: 400 feet up Pownal hill, minimal thereafter

This nice, long ride avoids traffic most of the way, except for a short time in Bennington. At Barber's Pond, on a back road to Bennington, there is a beautiful cross-section of an esker, a sinuous ridge formed by glacial activity.

DESCRIPTION
Start riding north on Route 7, and follow it uphill after the Green Mountain Park. At the crest of the hill in Pownal Center, take the only right (7.8 mi.) onto South Stream Road. As you approach Bennington you will encounter some forks; follow the roads that retain the double yellow lines and you should end up on Beech Street. At the Beech Street intersection with Route 9 (17.0 mi.) turn left onto Route 9. Follow signs through Bennington to Route 22 (26.5 mi.), then turn left onto Route 22 south and continue to the intersection with Route 346 (29.0 mi.). Take a left on Route 346, return to Pownal and continue to Williamstown.

MT. GREYLOCK
Distance: 35.4 miles
Estimated time: At least two to three hours
Elevation Change: 2,800 feet

This is unquestionably the steepest and most challenging ride in the Williamstown vicinity. Euphemistically, cyclists often call this an "extremely rewarding" ride. After entering the Mount Greylock Reservation, you ascend almost 3000 feet in 6.7 miles.

Despite the difficulties, this ride is breathtakingly beautiful, with stunning views from many points on the way to the summit, as well as from the summit itself. Vehicle traffic on both Notch and Rockwell Roads can be quite heavy, particularly in the summer and foliage seasons, so keep to one side of the road and stay alert.

DESCRIPTION
Ride east on Route 2, take a right on Luce Road (1.5 mi.) and bear left as it becomes Pattison Road. Just past the reservoir, bear right onto Notch Road and continue to the Mount Greylock State Reservation (5.3 mi.). From the entrance, climb steeply to the intersection of Notch and Rockwell Roads (11.3 mi.), and take Rockwell Road to the summit (12.0 mi.).

After you are finished catching your breath and admiring the view, follow Rockwell Road down the south side of the mountain. The road descends first steeply and then more gradually to intersect Route 7 just north of Lanesboro (20.4 mi.). To complete the loop, ride north on Route 7 to Williamstown (35.4 mi.).

FLY-FISHING

> All streams are talkative, and a hill stream is the greatest
> chatterer of all. It is never boring, yet always soothing. It is
> a thousand voices in one, and one voice in a thousand. Do
> not think as you lie beside it, but let it think for you. Then
> you will hear the voice and message of the hill.
>   - Frank Smythe

Williamstown and the surrounding areas offer some of the most
productive fly-fishing in Massachusetts. The Green River, Hoosic
River and smaller tributaries flow through town, and the Deerfield
River is only a short drive away. These waterways have many accesses for excellent fishing in all but the coldest months of the
year. Brown, rainbow, and brook trout inhabit these waters.

Several fishing accesses are marked with a fish icon on the
North Berkshire Trails map. Many of these are protected by the
Massachusetts Division of Fisheries and Wildlife.

EQUIPMENT

Before purchasing a fishing rod or any other equipment, you
should talk to an experienced friend or salesperson. There are
many excellent books about tackle and fishing paraphernalia. If
you would like to gain some experience before buying your own
equipment, contact the Williams Outing Club for more information about fishing trips in the local area. WOC members may use
club equipment if they possess a current fishing license.

LICENSES

A fishing license must be purchased every year and displayed
visibly when in the field. A license is only valid in the state where
it is purchased, so be careful about straying into Vermont from
Williamstown. Massachusetts licenses can be obtained at the Williamstown Town Hall, located at 31 North Street (Route 7) just
north of Field Park.

CATCH-AND-RELEASE

Please practice catch-and-release fishing wherever you fish. Some important guidelines to remember are:

- Use barbless hooks to facilitate releasing the fish and minimize damage to the jaws.
- If you use a net, use a fine mesh to avoid damaging fins.
- Wet your hands before handling the fish.
- When removing a hook, keep the fish as close to the water as possible.
- After removing the hook, place the fish gently in moving water facing upstream.
- Keep a firm (but not too tight) hold on the fish until it is strong enough to swim away.

Using these guidelines, you should be able to have a great time without disturbing the fragile river ecosystem.

GREEN RIVER

The Green River holds many small brown, rainbow, and brook trout between six and thirteen inches in length; occasionally a lucky or skilled person can catch one as long as fifteen inches. These fish are very healthy and always put up a good fight. Spring and summer are the prime fishing times on the Green River because of the abundant fly hatches.

During this period, a brown or rainbow trout may jump clear out of the water for a fly that looks only remotely similar to a natural fly. In general, the trout in the Green River are not very selective, making the river a great one for the beginning angler.

HOW TO GET THERE

- The Green River runs parallel to Water Street (Route 43), and can be fished almost anywhere you can park your car. Please heed all "No Trespassing" signs and do not cross private property unless you have the landowner's permission.
- One particularly accessible area is Mt. Hope Park, located 3 miles south of the intersection of Route 2 and Water Street.
- The Massachusetts Division of Fisheries and Wildlife main-

tains an access point at the entrance to Mt. Hope Farm, south
of Mt. Hope Park along Route 43.

RECOMMENDED FLIES
- Elk Hair Caddis (size 12-16)
- March Brown (size 12-16)
- Adams (size 14-18)
- Hare's Ear Nymph (size 10-16)
- Pheasant Tail Nymph (size 14-16, for big fish)
- Muddler Minnow (any size, in bigger pools)

HOOSIC RIVER

As the water level on the Green River decreases during the hot
summer months, the Hoosic River becomes a particularly attractive
fishing spot. The Hoosic's two branches run from Clarksburg and
Cheshire, meet in North Adams and continue through Williamstown into Pownal, Vermont and finally into New York.

While not as easily accessible as the Green River, the Hoosic
River holds some of the area's biggest brown and rainbow trout,
ranging in size from fourteen to twenty-three inches. Since a fish
rising is a rarity on the Hoosic, nymph and streamer fishing is
most common.

Below North Adams, do not eat any of the Hoosic River trout,
as they may contain high levels of Polychlorinated Biphenyls
(PCBs) and heavy metals that are suspected of being highly car-
cinogenic. Please release all Hoosic River fish!

HOW TO GET THERE
- There are many access points along the Hoosic. Refer to the
  North Berkshire Trails map to find the trails, canoe access and
  fishing access points indicated.

RECOMMENDED FLIES
- Hare's Ear Nymph (size 12)
- Black Wooly Worm (size 6-10)
- Black Marabou Muddler (size 4-10)
- Other assorted dark streamers

OTHER LOCAL BROOKS

Hemlock Brook and Broad Brook are two of the larger streams that empty into the Hoosic River. The Massachusetts Division of Fisheries and Wildlife maintains several posted access points to Hemlock Brook along Routes 2 and 7 south of Williamstown (see *North Berkshire Trails* map).

Broad Brook is a breathtakingly beautiful stream choked with cobbles in White Oaks, north of Williamstown. Respect private property in the area and be conscious of the Vermont border near the Broad Brook trailhead (see map).

DEERFIELD RIVER

The Deerfield offers some of the best trout fishing in the entire northeast, in some of the most beautiful surroundings. It has a large population of both stocked and native brown, rainbow, and brook trout. During the spring and summer, the Deerfield offers great dry-fly fishing. It is particularly famous for its Caddis hatches.

Water levels may rise without warning for hydroelectric power generation, so always inquire about water release schedules before venturing to the river. Visit www.zoaroutdoor.com/schedule.htm for scheduled release dates, and www.h2oline.com for flow predictions. A water level of 75-150 cubic feet per second is ideal for fishing. Levels of 700 CFS and above can be dangerous.

For more information on fishing the Deerfield refer to *The Deerfield River Guidebook*.

HOW TO GET THERE

- From the junction of Routes 2 and 7, take Route 2 east towards North Adams.
- Follow Route 2 past North Adams up and over the famous "hairpin." Turn at first left after the bronzed elk historical marker onto Whitcomb Hill Road at 12.6 miles.
- Follow the steep winding Whitcomb Hill Road all the way to the end, turn left onto River Road heading towards Monroe.
- Follow River Road for 2.0 mi., bear right onto a road directing you to a catch-and-release fishing area. Park along the shoulder or at designated parking near outhouses. Look for trails leading a short walk to the put-in.

- This mile long stretch is the best area for fishing, but all fish must be handled very carefully and returned unharmed to the river.
- You can also take a right at the stop sign and drive five miles down river to the ZOAR campground, where parking is available for easy river access. This, however, is not a catch-and-release section; canoes and kayaks may interrupt your fishing.

RECOMMENDED FLIES

- Between May and August, an Elk Hair Caddis size 12-16 is always an effective fly for evening fishing.
- Other effective flies include small midges (size 18-24), and bead-headed nymphs.

Nate Lowe '96—Climbing in New Hampshire.

ROCK CLIMBING

Climbing moves outdoor recreation to the vertical plane where an array of technical skills must be learned for safe travel. Students interested in starting to climb should enroll in WOC classes or visit the Nate Lowe Memorial Climbing Wall in the Towne Field House. If you already have experience on rock, you will find that climbing in the North Berkshire area is limited to small crags that are rarely or poorly described because of unresolved access issues. Some bouldering, including a few excellent boulders, can be found near the junction of the Chestnut Trail and the Class of '98 Trail in Williamstown. Williams students should contact the Outing Club for information on Williamstown and other Berkshire County crags. The purpose of this section is to point you to more distant areas and resources to explore them on your own. All of the guides mentioned below may be borrowed from the WOC library.

Within a 1.5-hour radius are several larger crags for both top-roping and lead climbing. As access to these areas may change over time, please respect postings and property owners in the area.

FARLEY LEDGES
Location: Erving, MA
Driving time: 1 hour 20 minutes
Other info: Top-roping, lead climbing, bouldering. 100+ routes.

HOW TO GET THERE
- Drive east on Route 2 past I-91.
- Find the (unmarked) parking lot on the left, 3.3 miles past the junction with Rt. 63.

DESCRIPTION

Once you have found the parking lot, follow the well-marked trail up to a map of the crag. By request of the property owners, no published information on routes exists, so make sure to get a tour from someone who knows their way around if it is your first time there.

Please do not publish any information about routes, formally or otherwise, since this may lead to restrictions on access for everyone. More information on Farley Ledges can be found on MountainProject.com and on climbgneiss.org.

ROSE LEDGE

Location: Northfield Farms, MA
Driving time: 1 hour 20 minutes
Other info: Top-roping and lead climbing. 100+ routes, many new route possibilities.

HOW TO GET THERE

- Drive east on Route 2 past I-91.
- Turn north on Route 63 and drive approximately 1.5 mi.
- Turn right on Poplar Mt. Rd. and drive 0.2 mi. to a parking area on the left.
- There is a $3 car/$5 van fee for parking.

DESCRIPTION

The Rose Ledge Trail takes you to the base of the cliff in about 15 minutes. The Falcon Guide *Rock Climbing New England* has a section describing the Main Wall and Overhang Buttress. Information on Rose Ledge can also be found on MountainProject.com and climbgneiss.org.

CHAPEL LEDGE

Location: Ashfield, MA
Driving time: 50 minutes
Other info: Top-roping and lead climbing. 20+ routes, well maintained. Heed notices regarding bird-nesting areas.

HOW TO GET THERE

- Drive east on Route 2 to Route 8 south to Adams.
- Follow signs for Route 116 east. Route 116 will "T" into Route 116/112.
- Take a left, go 2 mi. to Ashfield, follow Route 116 right and go through town.
- 1.6 mi. past Ashfield, 116 bears sharply to the left. Go straight onto a road marked "Williamsburg 9 miles."
- 2.3 mi. along this road is a parking area on the right.

DESCRIPTION

A trail leads to the cliffs from the right side of the road. The crag is divided into the Main Slab, Aid Free Wall, the Roof, and the Upper Ledges. The Falcon Guide *Rock Climbing New England* has a section on Chapel Ledge. More information can also be found on MountainProject.com and climbgneiss.org.

Across the road from the parking area, a dirt road leads to a path to a nice swimming hole. The main attraction of this swimming hole is a 15 foot high natural water slide. Ask local climbers or the Williams Outing Club for more information.

NEW ENGLAND CLIMBING

Due to the lack of very large cliffs in the immediate vicinity, Williams climbers often range much farther afield. Most of the best climbing in the Northeastern United States is 2-4 hours from Williamstown.

The Shawangunks of southern New York State are perhaps the best known cliffs in the northeast. These beautiful quartz-pebble conglomerate cliffs demand climbing horizontal cracks and pulling through overhangs on big jugs. The "Gunks" are about a two and a half-hour drive southwest of Williamstown. Several guides exist for this area including *Shawangunks Rock Climbs* by Dick Williams. Information on the Gunks can also be found on MountainProject.com.

Also of note are the basalt cliffs of central Connecticut. Ragged Mountain is a very popular area a little over two hours away. The Falcon Guide *Rock Climbing New England* has a section on Traprock and Ragged Mountain, and *Traprock: Connecticut Rock Climbs,* by Ken Nichols, is another guide to the area. Information on Traprock and Ragged Mountain can also be found on MountainProject.com.

The White Mountains of New Hampshire provide many fantastic granite cliffs such as Cannon Mountain, Cathedral and Whitehorse ledges, and Rumney. Information on the White Mountains abounds; Ed Webster's *Rock Climbs in the White Mountains of New Hampshire* is a classic volume. The Falcon Guide *Rock Climbing New England* covers all of the major climbing areas in New Hampshire. *Rumney,* by Ward Smith, is an excellent guide to this popular sport climbing area. Information on climbing in New Hampshire can also be found on MountainProject.com.

In upstate New York, the Adirondacks are filled with good climbing, including some of the most remote and highest cliffs in the northeast. Towering cliffs of finger ripping anorthosite (an igneous rock) and other metamorphic rocks fill the area. *A Rock Climber's Guide to Adirondack Rock* by Jim Lawyer and Jeremy Haas provides a detailed guide to both rock and ice climbing in this area. Information on climbing in the Dacks can also be found on MountainProject.com.

NATE LOWE MEMORIAL CLIMBING WALL

In 1995 the Williams Outing Club dedicated a 2,000 square-foot climbing wall in memory of Nate Lowe '96, an avid outdoorsman responsible for designing the wall. Since then, hundreds of people in the Williams College community have used the artificial wall to learn the basics of climbing safety and technique from experienced and trained student instructor-monitors.

Limited semester-long Williamstown community memberships are offered in the spring and fall for a small fee. Membership allows access to the climbing wall for the duration of the semester.

PADDLING

The Berkshires offer many scenic and adventure-filled waterways, including several natural lakes and major rivers. Except for the nearby Hoosic River and Windsor Lake, most areas are a thirty-minute to one-hour drive from Williamstown.

Paddling is most easily enjoyed from early May to October. A favorite time of year is late September when trees cloaked in their autumn color line the banks, and high overhead geese squawk their farewells as they V southward.

Lakes tend to freeze up in January and thaw by late April. However, during this cold period extreme canoeing and whitewater paddling can still be found on some local river sections.

For enjoyable and safe boating, preparation and precaution are essential. Plan your route, including ground transportation, in advance. Dress for the weather, but be prepared for changes – carry extra clothing in a watertight bag. Bring a filled water bottle, quick energy foods, and sun block if necessary. An extra paddle can be helpful, and always travel with others if paddling on whitewater.

For more information, use the references in the bibliography of this book or contact the Williams Outing Club.

EQUIPMENT

As canoeing and kayaking have grown in popularity over the last thirty years, so has the difficulty in choosing a boat that best suits your needs among the great variety of models available. Call your local canoe/kayak supplier and find out when they have "demo" days. Test a variety of boat types until you find one that feels comfortable for your skill level. Talk to other boaters to hear their opinions on different designs. Experiment with paddles too, giving attention to length, weight, durability and expense.

When choosing a personal floatation device (PFD), a proper fit is most important. It should fit snugly around the torso so that it cannot be pulled over one's head. A PFD should also have Coast Guard ratings pertaining to body weight and intended use. It is highly recommended that PFDs be worn whenever paddling. It is a Massachusetts State law that vests be worn from September 15 – May 15.

Dry bags are rubberized, sealed closure bags that can be filled with extra clothing, food, first aid kit, cameras, and other personal items that need safeguarding from wetness. They should be connected to a canoe thwart to avoid loss during flips, or stuffed snugly inside a kayak's stern compartment. Dry bags can be purchased in stores that outfit water sports.

Aqua socks, strap-on rubber sandals, old sneakers or specialty water shoes are good for launching and getting out of boats. If you have wet shoes you are more willing to enter the water and avoid contorted and often dangerous attempts to keep your feet dry. They also provide protection and better footing on rugged rock-strewn river bottoms.

You will need a map and guidebook for put-in and take-out information. They often describe hazards such as dams, quick drops, whitewater and water fluctuations. Guides also generally give distance and time for sections paddled and sometimes include interesting natural history.

To transport a canoe or kayak you need a roof rack for your vehicle. Before setting out, make sure the boat(s) are safely secured to the transport vehicle. The bow, stern, and middle hull should all be tied down to prevent any movement while traveling.

Whitewater enthusiasts need specialized gear and training. For more information we recommend that you find books solely focused on this particular activity or enroll in whitewater boating classes. Contact the Williams Outing Club or your local outfitter for specific information and class offerings.

LAKES & PONDS

Lakes and ponds throughout Berkshire County and surrounding areas are great for canoe trips or practicing kayak skills for whitewater runs.

WINDSOR LAKE

Location: North Adams
Driving time: 15 minutes
Map location: R – 16

HOW TO GET THERE

- From the junction of Routes 2 and 7, follow Route 2 east.
- At 5.3 mi. the road splits, stay right and descend towards North Adams' town center and Main Street.
- Follow Main St. through a stop light across Route 8a and turn right at a rotary onto Church St. at 5.7 miles.
- Drive past the Massachusetts College of Liberal Arts.
- Take your next left onto Bradley Street at 6.4 mi. and ascend a steep hill to Historic Valley Park.

DESCRIPTION

Windsor Lake (known as Fish Pond to many locals) is a small, quiet body of water next to Historic Valley Park, an excellent place for beginner paddlers to learn and practice strokes. There is a beach for public swimming and a playground at the park for young children.

PONTOOSUC LAKE

Location: Pittsfield
Driving time: 30 minutes
USGS maps: Pittsfield East, MA & Pittsfield West, MA

HOW TO GET THERE

- From the junction of Routes 2 and 7, take Route 7 south.
- After driving along Pontoosuc Lake, turn right at a signal light onto Hancock Rd at 17.2 mi.
- Cross over the dam, in a short distance there will be an entrance on the right to public parking and a boat launch.

DESCRIPTION

This is a popular lake for motorboats and jet skis during the summer months. The fishing is good, and there is a swimming beach near the public entrance. Paddling is best during the dawn and dusk light, when the water is calm and quiet, and the sun is low, giving off radiant colors that play on the water.

ONOTA LAKE

Location: Pittsfield
Driving time: 35 minutes
USGS map: Pittsfield West, MA

HOW TO GET THERE

- From the junction of Routes 2 and 7, take Route 7 south towards Pittsfield.
- After driving along Pontoosuc Lake, turn right at a signal light onto Hancock Rd. at 17.2 miles.
- Follow Hancock Rd. and turn left onto Highland Ave. at 18.1 miles.
- Take Highland Ave. to its end. Go straight through signal light (when green!), Highland Ave. becomes Valentine Road.
- There will be a sign for Burbank Park, the public boat access and swimming area for Onota Lake at 19.8 miles.

DESCRIPTION

The **Taconic Range** forms a beautiful backdrop to the west of this large lake. Onota Lake is a great place to see a variety of waterfowl although it does tend to be busy with motorboats during the summer months. This is the home of the Williams College Crew Team that has a boathouse on the northeast shore. Regattas take place in the fall and spring. For more information concerning these races, please contact the Williams College Athletic Department.

GRAFTON LAKES

Location: Grafton, NY
Driving time: 25 minutes
USGS map: Grafton, NY

HOW TO GET THERE

- From the junction of Routes 2 and 7, follow Route 7 south.
- At 2.3 mi. turn right onto Route 2 (west) towards Troy, NY.
- Follow Route 2 to the town of Grafton, NY. Look for signs directing you to Grafton Lakes State Park at 15.8 miles.
- Enter the park and follow signs to designated boat launch area.

DESCRIPTION

Long Pond, one of four lakes in Grafton Park, is a favorite for canoeing or kayaking. It is a small body of water with big charm. Birches, beeches, and maples line the shore. Great blue herons stand like statues "wading" patiently for a meal to swim by, and Osprey fly silently above on spiraling currents of wind. This is a great paddle, especially in the fall when the water reflects a myriad of colors from the deciduous trees.

LAUREL LAKE

Distance: Lenox and Lee
Driving time: 45 minutes
USGS map: Stockbridge, MA

HOW TO GET THERE

- From the junction of Routes 2 and 7, take Route 7 south towards Pittsfield.
- Continue through Pittsfield on Route 7 south towards the town of Lee and the Mass Turnpike, follow signs to Route 20 east.
- Take Route 20 east past the Route 7 south intersection.
- Laurel Lake will be on the right side of the road. There is a large paved parking area with a boat launch at 28.5 miles.

DESCRIPTION

Laurel Lake is a great fishing and canoeing spot. There are also two beaches for swimming, one on the east shore, and another on the south shore. The lake has some very deep spots where large lake trout and land-locked salmon like to hang out.

STOCKBRIDGE BOWL

Location: Stockbridge
Driving time: 50 minutes
USGS map: Stockbridge, MA

HOW TO GET THERE

- From the junction of Routes 2 and 7, take Route 7 south towards Pittsfield and follow signs to Route 7A Lenox Center.
- Travel through town center, at Lenox monument turn right onto Route 183 south at 26.4 miles.
- Pass the famous Tanglewood music center on the left, stay on Route 183 south.
- A short distance past Tanglewood is Berkshire Country Day School, on the right side. Immediately after is a large public parking area and boat access on the left side at 28.8 miles. There is no sign, be careful not to miss the entrance.

DESCRIPTION

The bowl is another fine fishing, canoeing and swimming spot. It is a great place to boat with a picnic and listen to the wonderful sounds of a Tanglewood concert on a summer day or moonlit evening!

GOOSE POND

Location: Lee
Driving time: 1 hour
USGS map: East Lee, MA

HOW TO GET THERE

- From the junction of Routes 2 and 7, take Route 7 south towards Pittsfield.
- Continue through Pittsfield on Route 7 south towards the town of Lee and the Mass Turnpike, follow signs to Route 20 east.
- Take Route 20 east past the turnoff to the Turnpike, turn right onto Forest St. at 31.6 miles.
- Follow Forest St. until you come to a large grouping of mailboxes on the left side of the road and a state public fishing access sign directing you up a dirt road at 33.7 miles.
- At the top of a hill you will see the boat launch to your right. Please be respectful of the private property postings and park your vehicle along the posted fence or designated parking area.

DESCRIPTION

Goose Pond is a Berkshire jewel located in Lee, Massachusetts. It is made up of lower and upper sections. The lower section is surrounded by private land with many homes along the shore and tends to get busy with small powerboats. Paddle 1.5 mi. east to the upper section and you feel like you are in the middle of a true wilderness area. There is good fishing and great swimming to be found here.

The **Appalachian Trail** is nearby and a wonderful Appalachian Mountain Club cabin maintained for people travelling along the trail is located on the north shore shortly after entering the Upper Goose. Great blue herons, hawks, and beavers are just a few of the frequent visitors to this scenic spot.

Be cautious of the weather. Afternoon westerly winds can make paddling quite difficult on the lower section when returning to the boat launch.

SHERMAN RESERVOIR

Location: Borders Monroe, MA; Readsboro, VT; and Whitingham, VT
Driving time: 45 minutes
USGS map: Rowe, VT

HOW TO GET THERE

- From the junction of Routes 2 and 7, follow Route 2 east (13 mi.).
- Turn left on Whitcomb Hill Road (15.5 mi.).
- Left turn on River Road (22 mi.).
- Continue onto Readsboro Road (entering VT) (24.6 mi.).
- The parking area and boat lunch are on the right.

DESCRIPTION

A favorite paddling spot: great for birding and other wildlife sightings! Sherman Reservoir is easy to get to and has a picnic area near the boat launch. The reservoir is about two miles in length - plenty of distance to canoe and kayak. If you head north, the waterway eventually turns into a small creek. Heading south, you can go as far as the dam's warning buoys before reaching the dam wall. Swimming and fishing are plentiful. Be mindful of headwinds that can come on fast!

SOMERSET RESERVOIR

Location: Somerset, VT
Driving time: 1.5 hours
USGS map: Mount Snow, VT & Stratton Mountain, VT

HOW TO GET THERE

- From the junction of Routes 2 and 7, follow Route 7 north to Bennington.
- In Bennington take Route 9 east (right) at 13.0 mi.
- Follow Route 9 past the junction with Route 8 at 26.5 mi.
- 1.5 mi. beyond the junction look for a sign directing you to Somerset Reservoir and turn left onto Forest Road #71 at 28.0 mi.
- Forest Road quickly becomes a passable gravel/dirt road

for the next 9 miles and leads you directly to a public access on the south shore.

DESCRIPTION

This is truly a spectacular place for paddling. Nestled in a remote area surrounded by the Green Mountain National Forest, there is plenty of lake to canoe and kayak. Swimming and fishing are also plentiful. Be cautious of the weather, winds can pick up to quickly churn the water into white caps. Bear, moose, and eagles are some of the wildlife that may be seen in this area.

RIVERS

The Berkshire Hills are the headwaters of two beautiful meandering rivers, the Housatonic and the Hoosic. Both are of great recreational value and provide habitat for numerous species of wildlife. On the eastern boundary of Berkshire County, the Deerfield River flows south and east toward the Connecticut River. For whitewater paddling, sections of the Deerfield offer the best and most challenging rapids. The headwaters of the Westfield and Farmington rivers are also found in Berkshire County to the south. Neither is described here, but both offer recreational opportunities including whitewater.

HOOSIC RIVER
Location: Williamstown, MA & Pownal, VT
Distance: 5 to 20 minutes
USGS map: North Adams, MA & Pownal, VT

HOW TO GET THERE
Following are directions to five boat launch areas: one in North Adams, MA; two in Williamstown, MA; one in North Pownal, VT; and one in North Petersburgh, NY. The descriptions begin with the farthest upstream put-in and continue downstream. Paddlers can certainly choose to put in at any of these launch sites and take out at the next closest one. There is enough current and class 2 rapids to make paddling upstream difficult, so plan on doing a shuttle between put-in and take-out. The river is most navigable for canoes and kayaks when running at least 150-1000 CFS. CFS levels <150 make the river difficult to navigate due to shallow water. Levels >1000 result in very fast moving, challenging water best attempted by experienced paddlers only. To check water levels for sections of the Hoosic, visit waterdata.usgs.gov.

Ashton Avenue
- From the junction of Routes 2 and 7, drive east on Route 2 towards North Adams.
- At 2.3 mi. turn left onto Ashton Ave.
- Follow Ashton Ave. 0.2 mi. to a parking area located on the right.

Cole Field (Williams College athletic fields)
- Drive east on Route 2 from Field Park and turn left onto Park St. at 0.2 miles.
- Follow Park and turn right onto Lynde Lane at 0.5 miles.
- Follow Lynde a short distance and then turn left (north) onto Stetson Road at the tennis courts.
- Follow Stetson to Eph's pond and the playing fields.
- At 1.0 mile park to the left, along the barrier. Please do not block the gate or roadway.
- Follow the paved path north towards the river, past a small building to a signed gap in the bushes.

Waste Transfer Station - Lauren's Launch
- From the junction of Routes 2 and 7, take Route 7 north towards Pownal, VT.
- At 1.2 mi. turn left onto Williamstown Department of Public Works (DPW) road.
- Follow Simonds Rd. over a set of railroad tracks. Immediately past the road to the transfer station there will be a large parking area on the right at 1.4 miles. The put-in is directly across the parking area at the riverbank.
  Note: As of 2019, this is not a very established put-in or take-out. It is a steep bank to moving water that can make for a difficult entry or exit.

North Pownal, Vermont
(Take-out only; dam downstream within ½ mile)
- From the junction of Routes 2 and 7, follow Route 7 north towards Pownal, VT (4.2 mi.).
- Turn left onto Route 346 north (4.7 mi.).
- Follow Route 346 north, passing through a narrow cut between rock outcrops (6.8 mi.).

- Turn left onto Dean Rd. (7.1 mi.).
- Turn left after crossing railroad tracks, and follow a grassy gravel path down towards the river.
- Taking out above the dam is risky. HOORWA hopes to construct a public path (connecting a take-out above the dam to access below) sometime in the near future.

The 'Play Wave' on the Hoosic River
- From the junction of Routes 2 and 7, follow Route 7 north towards Pownal, VT.
- Turn left on Route 346 north (4.2 mi.).
- Follow Route 346 north, pass through a small community and bear left at the fork to continue following 346 north towards North Petersburgh, NY (7.7 mi.).
- Cross over the Hoosic River and enter into NY state (8.8 mi.).
- Continue 0.8 mi. There will be a gravel pull-out parking area on the left next to the railroad tracks. Park there. You can then carefully cross the active railroad tracks to access the river and Play Wave within 50 yards of the parking area.

The Play Wave is a hydraulic feature of the river created by a narrowing squeeze of the river banks with a short, quick ledge drop. The main tongue of the river continues in a short wave train with two strong eddies river right and river left. An experienced whitewater kayaker/canoer can move from either eddy to the initial wave after the drop and 'surf' the wave. This is most fun at river levels ranging between 125-700 CFS. The lower range (125-250 CFS) makes for an excellent learning to 'surf' opportunity. CFS of 250 and higher is more of a challenge, especially for beginners. Note that this is a shallow area: whitewater experience and gear is necessary, especially helmets! There is also a whirlpool eddy at the bottom of the wave train that, at higher water levels, can be very tricky to navigate and often flips boats! Overall, this can be an excellent park and play spot. Make sure to always paddle with others in whitewater situations.

DESCRIPTION
From its marshy beginning in Cheshire, Massachusetts, the Hoosic

River flows northwestward through Vermont and into New York State where it joins the Hudson River. It offers abundant wildlife and excellent fishing – though pollutants have rendered the fish inedible. Its meandering course makes for a wonderful paddle. The sections of the Hoosic this guide covers consist of flatwater with a few Class I and Class II whitewater stretches. To avoid low water levels, spring, early summer, and after heavy rains are the best times to paddle. There may be water hazards such as tree blowdowns that you should be watchful for.

From the Ashton Avenue put-in, the approximate paddling distances are: 2.4 mi. to Cole Field, 3.9 mi. to the Waste Transfer Station, and 12 mi. to the Pownal take-out.

HOUSATONIC RIVER

Location: Lenox and Lenoxdale
Driving time: 45 minutes
USGS map: Pittsfield East, MA and East Lee, MA

There are several great paddling sections of the Housatonic River. The following is a favorite of the Williams Outing Club.

HOW TO GET THERE

- From the junction of Routes 2 and 7, take Route 7 south through Pittsfield.
- Turn left onto New Lenox Road at 23.5 miles.
- Follow through an intersection and over railroad tracks; just before crossing over the river, there will be a sign directing you into the John F. Decker boat launch on the right side of the road at 24.9 miles.
- Due to limited parking, please park in the adjacent lot to the west once you unload boats and gear.

DESCRIPTION

The Housatonic River begins in the Berkshire Hills and winds its way 150 miles south where it empties into Long Island Sound. There are several excellent paddling forays that range from gentle meandering currents to exciting whitewater.

The section described here is a very enjoyable paddle past

farmlands and through protected state Fisheries and Wildlife land. It is a great place to watch for wildlife, especially birds during the migratory and nesting seasons. The looming October Mountain in the east presents a spectacular wall of color in the fall.

From the Decker launch, the river twists and turns gently for approximately six miles until it reaches Woods Pond. The current is almost negligible, although you can see aquatic plant life pointing downstream. It is very possible to paddle down and return upstream, or you can shuttle a car to the Woods Pond Take Out*. The Housatonic is boatable year-round except in a deep, deep freeze. This is a highly recommended trip, especially for beginners.

For more historical information and details about other paddling sections refer to *A Canoeing Guide for the Housatonic River in Berkshire County.*

*Woods Pond Take Out from Decker Launch

- Turn left onto New Lenox Rd., cross over railroad tracks and turn left at the stop sign onto East St. at 0.6 miles.
- Follow East St. to an intersection with Housatonic St. and turn left at 3.4 miles.
- Follow Housatonic St. to the end, turn left onto Willow Creek Rd. at 4.3 miles. There will be a large parking area in front of the old Lenox train station. The station has been converted into a wonderful model train museum. It is now called the Berkshire Scenic Railway Museum. Definitely worth a visit after a nice paddle.

DEERFIELD RIVER

Location: Fife Brook – Florida, Massachusetts
Driving time: 35 minutes
USGS map: North Adams, MA & Rowe, MA

There are several exciting sections of this river that range from Class I to Class V whitewater. The Fife Brook stretch has Class II and III rapids and is a popular section for WOC kayak instruction.

HOW TO GET THERE

- From the junction of Routes 2 and 7, take Route 2 East

towards North Adams.

- Follow Route 2 past North Adams up and over the famous "hairpin." Turn at first left after the bronzed elk historical marker onto Whitcomb Hill Road at 12.6 miles.
- Follow the steep winding Whitcomb Hill Road all the way to the end, turn left onto River Road heading towards Monroe.
- Follow River Road for 2.0 mi., bear right onto a road directing you to a catch-and-release fishing area. Park along the shoulder or at designated parking near outhouses. Look for trails leading a short walk to the put-in.
- If shuttling with a vehicle, follow River Road downstream 4.9 miles. Immediately after the Zoar Gap bridge is a parking area on the left, and picnic area on the right. This is a good place to check out the class III rapids of Zoar Gap.

DESCRIPTION

From its beginnings in the Green Mountains, this once wild river, now tamed by a series of dams, runs southeastward until it meets up with the Connecticut River.

River flow policies have been established to create a consistent release calendar that benefits fishermen and boaters. This has caused a surge in the river's recreational popularity. The Deerfield is considered one of the best whitewater runs in the northeast when the dams let loose. Visit www.zoaroutdoor.com/schedule. htm for release dates, and www.h2oline.com for flow predictions.

Two sections in particular are best for whitewater excitement. The Fife Brook run is made up of mainly class I and II rapids. There is a challenging class III stretch through the Zoar Gap approximately five miles downstream from the put-in. If paddling this for the first time, scout the gap before entering.

Another exciting section is #5 Development, Monroe Bridge (known locally as the Dryway). It is popular among experienced paddlers, and is classified as a Class III and IV run. This section is most navigable by canoes and kayaks when water levels are between 800-1200 CFS. Levels <750 make for difficult navigation due to shallow water and running aground on rocks. >1300 CFS leads to challenging, fast-moving whitewater suited best for experienced paddlers. It is just north of the Fife Brook dam. For more detailed information about this section and others on the Deerfield River refer to *The Deerfield River Guidebook*.

BIBLIOGRAPHY

STARTING OUT & OUTDOOR TRAVEL

Drury, Jack K. et. al. *The Backcountry Classroom 2nd ed.* Guilford, CT. Falcon/Globe Pequot Press, 2005.

Kjellstrom, Bjorn. *Be Expert with Map and Compass.* Macmillan General Reference, 1994.

Hampton, Bruce and David Cole. *Soft Paths: How to Enjoy the Wilderness Without Harming It* 3rd ed. Mechanicsburg, PA. Stackpole Books, 2003.

McGiveny, Annette. *Leave No Trace: A Guide to the New Wilderness Ethic* 2nd ed. Seattle, WA. Mountaineers Books, 2003.

Meyer, Kathleen. *How to Shit in the Woods.* Berkeley, CA. Ten Speed Press, 1989.

Petzoldt, Paul and Raye Carleson Ringholz. *The New Wilderness Handbook.* New York. W.W. Norton & Company, 1984.

Randall, Glen. *The Outward Bound Map and Compass Handbook.* New York. Lyons Press, 1998.

Claudia Pearson, editor. *NOLS Cookery* 5th ed. Mechanicsburg, PA. Stackpole Books, 2004.

FIRST AID

Hubbel, Frank R. *Wildcare.* Conway, NH. Stonehearth Open Learning Opportunities, 2014.

Isaac, Jeff and David Johnson.*Wilderness and Rescue Medicine* 3rd ed. Portland, ME. Wilderness Medical Associates, 2008.

Isaac, Jeff and Peter Goth. *The Outward Bound Wilderness First Aid Handbook.* New York. Lyons and Burford, 1991.

Schimelpfenig, Todd. *NOLS wilderness medicine.* Mechanicsburg, PA. Stackpole Books, 2006.

Tilton, Buck. *Backcountry First Aid and Extended Care* 5th ed. Guilford, CT. Globe Pequot Press, 2007.

Wilkerson, James A. *Medicine for Mountaineering & Other Wilderness Activities.* Seattle, WA. Mountaineers Books, 2001.

HISTORY

Brooks, Robert R.R., ed. *Williamstown: The First 250 Years 1753-2003.* Williamstown Historical Commission, 2005.

Burns, Deborah E. and Lauren R. Stevens. *Most Excellent Majesty: A History of Mount Greylock.* Pittsfield, MA. Berkshire Natural Resources Council, 1988.

Carney, William. *A Berkshire Sourcebook.* Pittsfield, MA. Junior League of Berkshire County, 1976.

Giller, Jeremy. "A Brief History of the Williams Outing Club," Williamstown, MA. 1993.

Livingston, Mark "A Portraiture of Stone Hill: Lying Between Green River and Hemlock Brook in Williamstown." Williamstown, MA. Williams College Center for Environmental Studies, 1972.

Perry, Arthur L. *Origins in Williamstown.* 1894.

Sacks, Bill "Williams Outing Club History." http://wso.williams.edu/orgs/woc, 2002.

Williams Outing Club, "The Blaze." Spring 1956.

"The 1931-1932 Season of the Williams Outing Club." (anon., yearbook memorandum).

Williams Outing Club Archives.

NATURAL HISTORY

Hendricks, Bartlett. *Birds of Berkshire County.* Pittsfield, MA. The Berkshire Museum, 1994.

Kricher, John. *A Field Guide to Eastern Forests.* Boston, MA. Houghton Mifflin, 1988.

Laubach, René. *A Guide to Natural Places in the Berkshire Hills.* Stockbridge, MA. Berkshire House Publishers, 1992.

Marchand, Peter. *North Woods: An Inside Look at the Nature of Forests in the Northeast.* Boston, MA. Appalachian Mountain Club Books, 1987.

Newcomb, Lawrence. *Newcomb's Wildflower Guide.* Boston, MA. Little, Brown and Company, 1989.

Strauch, Joseph, G., Jr.*Wildflowers of the Berkshires and Taconic Hills.* Stockbridge, MA. Berkshire House Publishers, 1995.

Weatherbee, Pamela. *Flora of Berkshire County Massachusetts.* The Berkshire Museum, 1996.

Williams Naturalists. *Farms to Forest: A Naturalist's Guide to the Ecology and Human History of Hopkins Memorial Forest.* Williamstown, MA. Center for Environmental Studies, 1995.

GUIDES TO TRAILS IN BERKSHIRE COUNTY

Appalachian Mountain Club. *Massachusetts Trail Guide*, 8th ed. Boston, MA. Appalachian Mountain Club Books, 2004.

Henry, Edward. *Berkshire and Taconic Trails: A Rangers Guide*, Hensonville, NY. Black Dome Press, 2008.

League of Woman Voters. *Runner's Guide to Williamstown.* Williamstown, MA.

Ryan, Christopher J. *Guide to the Taconic Trail System.* Amherst, MA. New England Cartographics, 1989.

Smith, Charles W.G. *Nature Walks in the Berkshire Hills.* Boston, MA. Appalachian Mountain Club Books, 1997.

Stevens, Lauren R. *50 Hikes in the Berkshire Hills.* Woodstock, VT. Countryman Press, 2016.

Stevens, Lauren R. *Hikes and Walks in the Berkshire Hills* 3rd ed. Woodstock, VT. Countryman Press, 2004.

Taconic Hiking Club. *Taconic Crest Trail Guide.* Albany, NY. Taconic Hiking Club, 2006.

Williams Outing Club. *WOC Trail Guide and Map*, 9th ed. Williamstown, MA. Williams Outing Club, 1999.

Williams Trail Commission. *The Mountains of Eph: A Guidebook of the Williams Outing Club.* Williamstown, MA. Williams Outing Club, 1927.

GUIDES TO TRAILS IN NEW ENGLAND

Appalachian Mountain Club. *AMC White Mountain Guide*, 28th ed. Boston, MA. Appalachian Mountain Club Books, 2007.

Appalachian Trail Conservancy. *Appalachian Trail Guide to Massachusetts and Connecticut*, 11th ed. Harper's Ferry, WV. 2000.

Brady, John and Brian White. *Fifty Hikes in Massachusetts.* Woodstock, VT. Backcountry Publications, 1983.

Dartmouth Outing Club. *The Dartmouth Outing Guide.* Hanover, NH. 1999.

Goodwin, Tony, ed. *Guide to Adirondack Trails: High Peaks Region*, 12th ed. Series. Adirondack Mountain Club. 1992.

Green Mountain Club. *Long Trail Guide*, 26th ed. Waterbury Center, VT. 2007.

Green Mountain Club. *Day Hiker's Guide to Vermont*, 5th ed. Waterbury Center, VT. 2006.

Mikolas, Mark. *Nature Walks in Southern Vermont*. Boston, MA. Appalachian Mountain Club, 1995.

Perry, John and Jane Greverus Perry. *The Sierra Club Guide to the Natural Areas of New England*. San Fransisco, CA. Sierra Club Books, 1990.

WINTER

Fredston, Jill A. and Doug Fesler. *Snow Sense* 5th ed. Anchorage AK. Alaska Mountain Safety Center, Inc., 1999.

Goodman, David. *Classic Backcountry Skiing*. Boston, MA. Appalachian Mountain Club Books, 1989.

Gorman, Stephen. *AMC Guide to Winter Camping*. Appalachian Mountain Club, 1991.

O'Bannon, Allen and Mike Clelland. *Allen and Mike's Really Cool Backcountry Ski Book*. Evergreen, CO. Chockstone Press, 1996.

Parker, Paul. *Free-Heel Skiing*, 3rd ed. Seattle, WA. Mountaineers Books, 2001.

Stevens, Lauren R. *Skiing in the Berkshire Hills*. Stockbridge, MA. Berkshire House Publishers, 1991.

BIKING

Bridge, Raymond. *Bike Touring: The Sierra Club's Guide to Outings on Wheels*. San Francisco, CA. Sierra Club Books, 1987.

Cuyler, Lewis C. *Bike Rides in the Berkshire Hills*. Stockbridge, MA. Berkshire House Publishers, 1991.

Duling, Sandy. *Short Bike Rides, Vermont*. Old Saybrook, CT. The Globe Pequot Press, 1997.

Immler, Robert M. *The Mountain Biker's Guide to Ski Resorts*. Woodstock, VT. Backcountry Publications, 1998.

Williams Outing Club. *WOC Bicycling Guide and Map*. Williamstown, MA. WOC, 1981.

FISHING

Hughes, Dave. *Reading the Water: A Fly Fisher's Handbook for Finding Trout in All Types of Water*. Mechanicsburg, PA. Stackpole Books, 1988.

Hughes, Dave. *Tactics for Trout*. Mechanicsburg, PA. Stackpole Books, 1990.

Lessels, Bruce and Norman Sims. *The Deerfield River Guidebook*. North Amherst, MA. New England Cartographics, 1993. (Fishing section by Jim Dowd).

Meck, Charles R. *Fishing Small Streams With a Fly Rod.* Woodstock, NY. Countryman Press, 1991.

O'Reilly, Pat. *River Trout Fishing: Expert Advice for Beginners (Fishing Facts).* North Pomfret, VT. Trafalgar Square, 1992.

CLIMBING

Cox, Steven M., Kris Fulsaas, ed. *Mountaineering: The Freedom of the Hills,* 7th ed. Seattle, WA. Mountaineers Books, 2003.

Long, John. *How to Rock Climb,* 4th ed. Evergreen, CO. Chockstone Press, 2003.

Powers, Phil. *NOLS Wilderness Mountaineering 2nd ed.* Mechanicsburg, PA. Stackpole Books, 2000.

Webster, Ed. *Rock Climbs in the White Mountains of New Hampshire.* Eldorado Springs, CO. Mountain Imagery, 1996.

PADDLING

Appalachian Mountain Club. *AMC River Guide: Massachusetts, Connecticut, Rhode Island* 4th ed. Boston, MA. Appalachian Mountain Club Books, 2006.

Appalachian Mountain Club. *AMC River Guide: New Hampshire and Vermont* 4th ed. Boston, MA. Appalachian Mountain Club Books, 2007.

Bechdel, Les and Slim Ray. *River Rescue,* 3rd ed. Boston, MA. Appalachian Mountain Club Books, 1997.

Berkshire County Regional Planning Commission and Housatonic Valley Association. *A Canoeing Guide for the Housatonic River in Berkshire County.*

Borton, Mark C., ed. *The Complete Boating Guide to the Connecticut River.* Woodstock, VT. Backcountry Publications, 1985.

Lessels, Bruce and Norman Sims. *The Deerfield River Guidebook.* North Amherst, MA. New England Cartographics, 1993.

Northeast Paddlers Message Board: Helpful information to find fellow paddlers, gear sales, and to discover what water is running. http://www.npmb.com

RESOURCES

EQUIPMENT AND SUPPLIES

The Spoke Bicycles
Bicycle equipment, repair and service.
Colonial Shopping Center • Williamstown, MA 01267
(413) 458-3456 • www.spokebicycles.com

Wild Oats Community Market
Non-profit consumers' cooperative food market.
Natural, organic and bulk foods.
320 Main Street • Williamstown, MA 01267
(413) 458-8060 • www.wildoats.coop

Berkshire Outfitters
Outdoor equipment, repairs and service.
Paddlesports and nordic skiing.
169 Grove Street • Adams, MA 01220
(413) 743-5900 • www.berkshireoutfitters.com

The Arcadian Shop
Outdoor clothing, equipment and service.
91 Pittsfield Road • Lenox, MA 01240
(313) 637-3010 • www.arcadian.com

AT Bicycle Works and Outfitters
144 Church Street • Cheshire, MA 01225
(413) 743-2453

Mike's Bike Shop
555 North Street • Pittsfield, MA 01201
(413) 443-1166

Ski Fanatics
Alpine ski equipment.

145 North Main Street • Lanesboro, MA 01237
(413) 443-3023 • www.skifanatics.com

Nature's Closet
61 Spring Street • Williamstown, MA 01267
(413) 458-7909 • www.naturescloset.net

BOOKSTORES

Chapter Two Books
Not-for-profit, used bookstore with adventure and travel literature.
37 Spring Street • Williamstown, MA 01267
(413) 884-4419

The Williams Bookstore
Full service bookstore with outdoor literature.
81 Spring Street • Williamstown, MA 01267
(413) 458-8071 • www.bkstr.com/williamsstore

The Mountaineers
Member-supported club with active outing, instructional and publishing departments.
7700 Sand Point Way NE • Seattle, WA 98115
(206) 521-6000 • www.mountaineers.org

LOCAL ORGANIZATIONS AND GOVERNMENT AGENCIES

Appalachian Mountain Club: Massachusetts AT Management Committee
Manages Adopt-a-Trail and volunteer trail crews, conducts educational programs and publishes information on the area.
www.amcberkshire.org/AT or contact AT@amcberkshire.org

Center for Environmental Studies
For information about Hopkins Memorial Forest.
55 Mission Park Drive • Williams College • Williamstown, MA 01267
(413) 597-2346 • ces.williams.edu

Department of Conservation and Recreation
For information about outdoor recreation in Berkshire County.

West Region • 740 South Street • Pittsfield, MA 01202
(413) 442-8928 • mass.gov/dcr

Massachusetts Division of Fisheries and Wildlife
Conservation of land for protection of wildlife.
Western District Office • 88 Old Windsor Road • Dalton, MA 01226
(413) 447-9789 • mass.gov/orgs/division-of-fisheries-and-wildlife

Hoosic River Watershed Association
Works to protect, preserve and restore the Hoosic River and surrounding watershed.
P.O. Box 667 • 906 Main St. • Williamstown, MA 01267
(413) 458-2742 • www.hoorwa.org

Pleasant Valley Wildlife Sanctuary
Massachusetts Audubon Society
472 W. Mountain Road • Lenox, MA 01240
(413) 637-0320 • www.massaudubon.org

New York Department of Environmental Conservation (DEC)
Owns and manages land along the Taconic Crest.
625 Broadway FL 5 • Albany, NY 12233
(518) 402-9405 • www.dec.ny.gov

Taconic Hiking Club
For information about the Taconic Crest Trail.
c/o R.J. Hydorn • 2 Miller Ave. • Troy, NY 12180
www.taconichikingclub.org

Town of Williamstown
Town Hall
31 North St. • Williamstown 01267
(413) 458-3500 • www.williamstown.net

The Trustees of Reservations
A private nonprofit member organization dedicated to preserving properties of exceptional scenic, historic, and ecological value.
www.thetrustees.org

Williams Outing Club
Williams College student outdoor organization.
39 Chapin Hall Drive • Williamstown, MA 01267
(413) 597-2317 • woc.williams.edu

Williamstown Rural Lands Foundation
Non-profit, member-supported Land Trust for the Williamstown area.
671 Cold Spring Road • Williamstown, MA 01267
(413) 458-2494 • www.wrlf.org

OTHER ORGANIZATIONS

Adirondack Mountain Club
A non-profit membership organization dedicated to conservation, recreation and education in the Adirondack Mountains. Maintains trails, lean-tos, huts and lodges. Publishes books and maps.
814 Goggins Road • Lake George, NY 12845
(800) 395-8080 • www.adk.org

Americorps
National service opportunities to meet critical needs in education, the environment, public safety, homeland security, and other areas.
1201 New York Avenue, NW • Washington, DC 20525
(202) 942-2677 • www.americorps.gov

Appalachian Mountain Club
A non-profit membership organization. Maintains huts, lodges and trails throughout the northeast for public use. Publishes books and maps for outdoor adventures in the eastern U.S.
10 City Square • Boston, MA 02129
(617) 523-0655 • www.outdoors.org

Appalachian Trail Conservancy
Coordinating body for Appalachian Trail management. Publishes a series of ten guidebooks for the trail.
P.O. Box 807 • Harper's Ferry, WV 25425
(304) 535-6331 • www.appalachiantrail.org

Green Mountain Club
A membership organization that maintains and protects the Long Trail and other hiking byways in Vermont.
4711 Waterbury-Stowe Rd. • Waterbury Center, VT 05677
(802) 244-7037 • www.greenmountainclub.org

Leave No Trace - Center for Outdoor Ethics
An organization that teaches people to enjoy the outdoors responsibly.
P. O. Box 997 • Boulder, CO 80306
(800) 332-4100 • www.lnt.org

National Outdoor Leadership School (NOLS)
A wilderness-based, non-profit school focusing on leadership and skills.
284 Lincoln St. • Lander, WY 82520
(800) 710-6657 • www.nols.edu

Outward Bound USA
Wilderness courses designed to inspire self-esteem, self-reliance, concern for others and care for the environment.
910 Jackson St., Suite 140 • Golden, CO 80401
(866) 467-7651 • www.outwardbound.org

SCA
Expense-paid conservation internships
4245 North Fairfax Drive, Suite 825 • Arlington, VA 22203
(703) 524-2441 • www.thesca.org

SOLO Wilderness Medicine
Offers courses in Wilderness Medicine from First Aid to WEMT.
P.O Box 3150
Conway, NH 03818
(603) 447-6711 • www.soloschools.com

U.S. Geological Survey Information Services
USGS Maps, realtime environmental data
Box 25286 - Denver, CO 80225
(888) 275-8747 • www.usgs.gov

Wilderness Medical Associates
"Providing the highest quality medical training to people who work or play in remote areas."
1 Forrest Ave. • Portland, ME 04101
(207) 730-7331 • www.wildmed.com

Wilderness Medicine Institute
Providing quality education for the recognition, treatment and prevention of wilderness emergencies.
National Outdoor Leadership School
284 Lincoln Street • Lander, WY 82520
(800) 710-6557 • www.nols.edu/wmi

Zoar Outdoor
Premier paddling school, outfitter shop and more.
7 Main Street • Charlemont, MA 01339
(413) 339-4010 • www.zoaroutdoor.com

INDEX